WILD HORSES
of the world

hamlyn

WILD HORSES of the world

MOIRA C. HARRIS

Foreword by HRH The Princess Royal

Photography by Bob Langrish

An Hachette UK Company
www.hachette.co.uk

First published in Great Britain in 2009 by
Hamlyn, a division of Octopus Publishing Group Ltd
2–4 Heron Quays, London E14 4JP
www.octopusbooks.co.uk
www.octopusbooksusa.com

Distributed in the U.S. and Canada by Octopus Books USA:
c/o Hachette Book Group USA
237 Park Avenue
New York NY 10017

ISBN: 978-0-600-61813-3

A CIP catalogue record of this book is available from the British Library.

Printed and bound in China

10 9 8 7 6 5 4 3 2 1

Contents

FOREWORD

Anybody who is interested in horses, in all their forms, will know of Bob Langrish because they will have seen his work. I have certainly known of his photographs and books throughout my competitive career. All his work reflects his understanding of horses and their environment and his experience and skill have brought equines to a wider and wider audience. In this book, we are reminded that horses

have a global and historical significance to man. Bob highlights that some of these breeds are now rare breeds because their contribution to human development has largely been overtaken by technology. But these equines still add value to all our lives and I hope that this book will help us to appreciate more clearly that horses are more than just pretty pictures.

Anne

HRH The Princess Royal

LEFT *At all stages of her life, HRH The Princess Royal has shared a magical connection with the horse.*

WILD HORSES: *their past, present and future*

Most of us feel a genuine connection with the wild horse, and it is easy to see why people who are not equestrians, or even horse-lovers, find the idea of free-living horses appealing. Many conjure up visions of a herd surging over open country: a sea of rippling coats, slender legs and waving manes. It is a romantic picture, although probably not very realistic.

Yet wild horses are beautiful. They are the perfect example of an animal crafted by nature for survival in the wilderness. Over generations, they have been engineered by their environment to be ideally suited for life there. What a marvel: to be hardy enough to gain nourishment from meagre forage, intelligent enough to find safety from the elements, cunning enough to outwit predators, and robust enough to live and die under the same sky.

Beyond the horse's outward beauty, most people would point to a more intangible quality: a spirit of freedom that exists deep under hide and mane. We admire the animals' indomitable will, which shuns domestic trappings to eke out an existence as their ancestors did centuries before. We have good reason to be envious of creatures that are living by their own wits, relying on instinct and surviving in the present; these are things that do not exist in our modern urbanized world.

Despite this admiration, the wild horse has had a tenuous relationship with humans through the ages. It has come a long way in recent history, yet in some cases it still has far to go. It was not long ago that any ownerless horse was eradicated, culled, exterminated – destroyed. However, thanks to the efforts of horse-lovers the world over, its fortunes are changing. Even so, for some wild horse breeds, it may be too late. Others are safe – for now. Until all of humankind realizes that its success as a race directly relates to its treatment of the world's animals, wild horses will always be in a precarious position.

LEFT *Abaco Barbs are the most endangered wild horses on the planet, with fewer than 15 left now.*

THE ORIGINS *of the horse*

The association of horses with humans has often been uncertain, even, by all accounts, when the horse was barely a horse. The horse originated on the North American continent, beginning with *Hyracotherium*, better known as *Eohippus* or the 'dawn horse'.

The dawn horse

This was a dog-sized animal that lived during the Eocene epoch, 55 to 45 million years ago. *Eohippus* was a shy, fast-moving and agile creature, running on five toes and eating the leaves of the plants growing in the jungles and swamps. It was hunted for meat by the Cro-Magnon people, but was one of the more gentle-natured creatures of the age. This may be why the horse eventually came to mean much more to people than simply a food source.

The dawn horse was an ancestor of *Equus caballus*, the first 'true horse', which came into existence about 4 million years ago, born out of the new environment that had slowly emerged: grassland. This horse was no longer a browser, like a deer, but a grazer. It was larger, brawnier and galloped on one toe: the hoof.

The spread of the horse

During this vast time period, the horse migrated throughout the world, via the land bridges that existed during the Ice Age, from Alaska and along the Asiatic mountain chain, and from Asia to Europe and Africa. Until about 1 million years ago, *Equus* was found all

RIGHT *The* Eohippus *– or Dawn Horse – near right, bears little resemblence to the modern* Equus caballus, *whose nearest prehistoric relative was the* Pliohippus, *far right, who roamed the Earth 10 million years ago during the Pleistocene period.*

EOHIPPUS *58 million years ago*

MESOHIPPUS *40 million years ago*

over Africa, Asia, Europe, North America and South America, in enormous migrating groups that can be compared to North America's gigantic herds of bison or the huge migrations of wildebeest in Africa.

About 8,000 to 10,000 years ago, the horse inexplicably disappeared from its birthplace in North America. While this was partly due to hunting by *Homo sapiens*, there may have been other contributing factors, such as increasing volcanic activity, disease pandemics and environmental catastrophes.

Elsewhere though, equines flourished and evolved into four different types. The horse as we know it evolved in Europe and western Asia. In areas where pastureland was lush and nutritious, the horse grew larger, stronger and more powerful. In areas where forage was not as plentiful or nourishing, the horse stayed small and thrifty.

There were three other types of equine:

1 the donkey in the north
2 the zebra and quagga in the south
3 the onager in the Fertile Crescent of the Middle East.

The horse, however, was the most dominant, particularly because it had four sub-types:

1 the Asiatic wild horse
2 the forest horse
3 the tundra pony
4 the tarpan.

The tarpan was probably the most prolific of them all, and most modern-day European horses are descended from it. The Celtic pony is most probably the main ancestor of Britain's native ponies, although the forest horse did have some influence. The forest horse was the forebear of many draught breeds, while the tundra pony probably has several Arctic breeds to its credit, ranging from the Icelandic pony to the Shetland pony.

As for their original homeland, it was several centuries before horses returned to North America, in about AD 1500. With the Spanish explorers and conquistadors landing on both coasts and bringing with them a host of breeds, including the Spanish Barb, the Iberian Sorraia, the Jennet, the Garrano and others, the continent rapidly made up for lost time as the equine population burgeoned.

Today there are wild horses on nearly every continent, each with a unique history and attributes. Because their numbers have been drastically reduced over decades, it is even more vital to protect the ones that currently exist.

MERYCHIPPUS *25 million years ago*

PLIOHIPPUS *10 million years ago*

BEHAVIOUR *in the wild*

To see a band of horses in the wild is a special event, not only because it is becoming a rare occurrence, but also because it provides the opportunity to witness a unique social structure. Horses easily adapt to virtually all types of environments, from desert to Arctic climates, from mountainous terrain to swampy seashores, but one thing stays constant: the behaviour in the herd.

Life in the herd

The horse is a community-dweller and does not do very well when isolated from its own kind. It is not just to ease loneliness either: in order to survive, horses must get along as a group and stick together. Wild horses live in herds that break into smaller social groups, known as bands.

Typically, each band has one stallion (although there could also be a couple of less dominant stallions), up to 11 mares and their foals, weanlings and yearlings. Band members change over time as young animals are driven out, or as young stallions challenge older males for dominance. Since both colts and fillies leave the band in which they were born, most of the individuals in the band are not related. Members are very loyal to their bands, and stallions and mares will form long-term relationships.

There is a dominance hierarchy in the band, also known as a 'pecking order'. This is the ranking system that develops among horses when they live in close proximity. Pecking order determines which horses are most dominant or most subservient, which direct the behaviour of others, which eat and drink first, and so on. Horses can move up and down in the pecking order as members enter or leave the band.

The leader of the band

Many accounts of wild horses paint a picture of a bold stallion in charge of a vast harem of mares, but this is not entirely accurate. While the stallion does protect and guard his herd, the real leader is the 'lead mare', also called the 'boss mare' or 'alpha mare'. She is usually a mature female in her prime. She is the one with excellent instincts, leading the band to good grazing and water. Ever watchful, she will lead the flight if danger is present. Her memory also serves her well, as she can backtrack and navigate the herd's vast territory, taking the best routes to better forage or shelter.

If the lead mare is the 'brains' of the operation, then the stallion is the 'muscle'. He makes sure that the band stays together. He fends off any stallions that challenge

LEFT *Skyros ponies are small, but they are hardy enough to survive the harsh conditions of island life.*

ABOVE *With foals at their sides, wild mares are acutely alert, even when seemingly grazing at their leisure.*

his position and also fights off predators that attack weaker herd members. In contrast to the boss mare, who takes her position at the front of the herd, the stallion will always be at the rear, nipping at any stragglers and protecting them from would-be marauders. During the spring breeding season, a stallion will intensify his actions to keep his herd together, but once the mating season is over, he will settle down into his role of guardian. He marks his territory through 'stud piles' – manure piles and urination spots that serve as his calling card.

Foals and foaling

Most foals are born in late spring or early summer, with the gestation period usually lasting 11 months. A mare may be left behind the band while she is giving birth. Within hours of the birth, the newborn foal will struggle to its feet and begin to nurse. During the first few days the mare's milk is rich in protein and maternal antibodies that give the foal immunity from some diseases. This first milk is called colostrum. The number of antibodies in the colostrum decreases rapidly after the mare has foaled, as does the foal's ability to absorb them. A foal is usually able to trot beside its mother when it is only a couple of hours old but, during its first few days of life, it can be rather wobbly and unsteady.

Once the foal is able to travel – which can take as little as a day – both mare and foal will rejoin the band. Although a foal begins nibbling at forage at a very early stage, it still relies on its mother's milk for nourishment. Throughout the day, the foal will stop its activity, whether it is cavorting, investigating plants, socializing with other foals or sleeping – and head for its mother to nurse. Often, after some disturbance or band movement, the foal will initiate nursing by approaching its mother, which suggests that nursing also provides a sense of security.

The importance of status

In the wild, most young horses are allowed to stay with the herd until they are between 1 and 2 years of age, when they reach full sexual maturity. Studies of wild herds have shown that the herd stallion will usually drive out both young colts and young fillies. Equine behaviourists believe that this practice reduces the opportunity for inbreeding, so that the stallion does not breed with his own fillies.

Fillies usually leave their own band for another, changing bands a number of times over the following couple of years before joining a band permanently. Colts on the other hand, become bachelors. Bachelors live in unstable groups, but remain within predictable home ranges. Horses are very loyal to their home ranges, which are not exclusive territories that have to be defended, and many overlap to a degree.

The band stallion has a hard life: living on the edge of the band, staying out in all weather while the band

BELOW *A young, inexperienced colt may challenge the older band stallion, but the scuffle is often mere posturing.*

ABOVE *A mare may lash out at a stallion's advances, especially if she is not in season for breeding.*

finds shelter, and fending off predators and challenges from other stallions who wish to take over the band.

Any confrontation between stallions is usually resolved by ritual posturing and snorting. Nevertheless, genuine fighting does occur and injuries are common, although fatalities are rare. A lead stallion can be replaced by a stronger successor at any time. When a stallion is 'dethroned' he may take on a smaller band of mares, or if he is too old, he may join a bachelor band.

Daily life

Two important factors influence feral horse behaviour:

1 social organization

2 the nature of the home range.

The home range is the area that the horse covers in its search for food and water. The distance and speed that a horse travels in a day depend on the size of the home range and the quality of the forage. On open ranges, horses have been shown to travel up to 65–80 km (40–50 miles) in a day in search of watering holes. So, the distance that a grazing horse travels depends on the location of water, the availability of food and the time that it spends foraging. When forage is scarce, feral horses graze for up to 22 hours a day, searching for food. When forage is plentiful, the horses graze only at dawn and dusk, resting during the day.

When the herd is under stress, for example when a predator is stalking the band or the weather is very bad, the safest place to be is in the centre of the herd because this position offers the most protection from the elements and is further away from predators. This means that the stallion can punish any misbehaving members by expelling them from the band, either temporarily or permanently.

Wild horses are naturally wary. When approached, they will take fright and run for cover. Their natural defensive instinct is flight, although a stallion can show aggression if he fears his band is being threatened

Wild or feral?

With one exception, the horses featured in this book are technically feral and not wild. However, none of these horses has ever had any of the trappings of domestication. They were born in the wild from generations of free-roaming equines. Certainly their behaviour is that of wild animals.

The distinction between feral animals and wild animals can be regarded as largely political. It is more difficult to make a case for the protection of a domestic animal that has turned wild than for a truly wild animal, and this is what governments and other interest groups seem to prefer.

Technically speaking, the only true wild horse is the Przewalski horse of Mongolia (see pages 160–167). Other wild equines include the zebra, the wild ass and the onager. All other horses are domestic stock that happens to lead a free-living existence.

Zebras

Zebras live in several parts of Africa and have never been truly domesticated. In the past, they could be found in gigantic herds right across Africa; now endangered, their numbers have dwindled and they are restricted to just a few habitats: the grasslands, savannas, woodlands, thorny scrublands, mountains and coastal hills.

The zebra was the second species, after the asses, to diverge from the earliest proto-horses, around 4 million years ago. Many individuals have crossed the zebra with a horse to create the curious 'zorse' but this has been done strictly for human vanity and serves no purpose.

Zebras have their trademark stripes, which they bear like a unique fingerprint, as no two zebras have exactly the same striping. The striping pattern helps the zebra to camouflage itself in the grasslands. Zebras generally have white coats with black (or brown) stripes. However, some zebras are born all black with white

RIGHT *Grevy's zebra, found mainly in Kenya and Ethiopia, is the largest species of zebra.*

stripes, or mostly dark with the striped pattern only on part of their coats. They also have upright manes that blend light and dark hairs.

There are three species of zebra:

1 the plains zebra
2 the mountain zebra
3 Grevy's zebra.

They all have excellent hearing and eyesight and can run at speeds of up to 56 km/hour (35 miles/hour). They also have a powerful kick that can cause serious injury to a predator, such as a lion, hyena or African wild dog.

Grevy's zebra

Grevy's zebra (*Equus grevyi*) is believed to have been the first of all zebra species in existence. Some evidence shows that there may have even been zebras in North America during prehistoric times. Fossils discovered in Idaho have produced some controversial findings, some saying that the Hagerman horse (*Plesippus shoshonensi*), which lived during the Pliocene period, is more closely related to the zebra than to *Equus caballus*. Its conformation is very similar to that of a horse, but the skull and teeth bear more resemblance to Grevy's zebra. As a result, the Hagerman horse is also called the American zebra, or Hagerman zebra.

Grevy's zebra is the largest of the zebras, with a very upright mane and a long, mule-like head. It is found in the grasslands of Ethiopia and northern Kenya. Due to large-scale hunting and poaching for its beautiful coat, Grevy's zebra is one of the rarest species of zebra in existence and is classed as an endangered species.

Plains zebra

The plains zebra (*Equus quagga*, formerly *Equus burchelli*), is the most common of the zebras and there are about 12 sub-species found across much of southern and eastern Africa. Its conformation is pony-like, unlike the Grevy's zebra similarity to a mule. Its stripes are bolder and broader than the Grevy's, and they reach down to the belly and broaden over the croup and haunches, where they slope upward and over the hindquarters. In males they are jet black; in females they fade to brown. Its erect mane also bears stripes.

BELOW *Plains zebra are not as endangered as other zebra species, but are still affected by poaching and loss of habitat.*

ABOVE *The mountain zebra can be found on rocky, arid plateaus, as high as 2,000 m (6,500 ft) above sea level.*

Mountain zebra

The mountain zebra, also called the Cape mountain zebra (*Equus zebra*) or Hartmann's mountain zebra (*Equus hartmannae*), lives in the south-western part of Africa and also looks more like an ass than a horse. It has bold stripes and a unique dorsal stripe that bears a zip-like pattern towards the hindquarters and the dock of the tail; this is its most easily recognizable feature. The underbelly is creamy white, interrupted by a dark stripe that runs the length of the belly. There is a hanging flap of skin on the upper neck, called a dewlap, which is reminiscent of an Adam's apple. The mountain zebra is classed as an endangered species.

Many people wonder if the different species of zebra mingle and interbreed. Even when zebras live in the same ranges, they stick to their own species in the wild. This is mainly due to the difference in chromosome numbers: Grevy's zebra has 46 chromosomes; the plains zebra has 44 chromosomes and the mountain zebra has 32 chromosomes. This means that any mating between these species of zebra is unlikely to be successful: even if fertilization does take place, the foetus is often aborted or miscarried, and any offspring that are produced are usually hybrid or sterile.

Nevertheless, scientists have successfully crossed captive plains zebras with mountain zebras. The hybrid foals lacked the signature dewlap of the mountain zebra and resembled the plains zebra, apart from their larger ears and their hindquarters' pattern. Attempts to cross a Grevy's zebra stallion with mountain zebra mares resulted in a high miscarriage rate.

Quagga

The quagga was similar to the plains zebra, but differed from other zebras because, instead of being completely striped from end to end, it only bore stripes on the shoulder, neck and barrel, with those on the hindquarters and ribs fading to plain brown.

It was hunted for its meat and hides, and to eliminate it from competition with domestic African livestock. It is long extinct: the last wild quagga was killed on the African plains in the late 1870s and the last one in captivity died at an Amsterdam zoo in 1883. Because the world did not realize that the quagga might be a separate species from the zebra, it was hunted to extinction. DNA testing has since revealed that the quagga was indeed a variant of the plains zebra.

African wild ass

The African wild ass (*Equus asinus*) is thought to be the ancestor of the domestic donkey. It lives in the arid deserts of Africa's Eritrea, Ethiopia and Somalia, and until recently, Sudan, Egypt and Libya, and is well suited to this type of environment. Its digestive system is uniquely suited to the sparse, dry forage found in deserts. It can extract and utilize water from its food and therefore does not need to drink as often as other wild game. Because of the sparse distribution of vegetation, wild asses live in isolation from each other (except for mares and foals), unlike the tightly grouped herds of wild horses. However, they have very loud voices that can be heard for over 3 km (2 miles), which helps them to stay in contact with other asses over the extensive territory.

There are several sub-species of wild ass. Each one is the size of a large pony, with a short, smooth coat that is light grey to fawn in colour, fading quickly to white on the undersides and legs. In addition to zebra-type stripes, there is a slender, dark dorsal stripe, as well as a stripe across the shoulder. The legs have primitive markings and the mane is upright and bristly. Their large ears give them an excellent directional sense of hearing and also help to cool them down by radiating heat.

BELOW *The Somali wild ass, a sub-species of the African wild ass, displays zebra-like stripes on its legs.*

ABOVE *The hardy onager is naturally equipped to thrive in arid desert conditions.*

Onager

The onager (*Equus hemionus*), also called the Asian wild ass, dwells in the deserts of Mongolia, northern Iran, Tibet, India and Pakistan. *Onager* is an ancient Greek word for 'ass' that may derive from the Sumerian word *ansu*. It is possible that these words are also related to the Greek word *agros*, meaning 'field', from which we get farming terms such as 'agriculture' and 'acre', which may suggest that the ass was the earliest domesticated farm animal.

Like many other large grazing animals, the onager has lost a good deal of its habitat over the years due to over-hunting and encroaching civilization. Of the six sub-species, one is extinct and two are endangered. The kiang (*Equus kiang*), a Tibetan relative, was previously considered to be a sub-species of the onager (*Equus hemionus kiang*), but recent molecular studies indicate that it is a distinct species.

The onager is a little larger than a donkey and a little more horse-like. It is short-legged compared to horses, and its colouring varies with the season, but is generally pale, especially on the flanks, the face and the underside. The onager grows a dense winter coat, and the mane is often wispy and bristly. It has short legs and small hooves, and the tail is short with a tuft of very long hairs at the tip.

North America

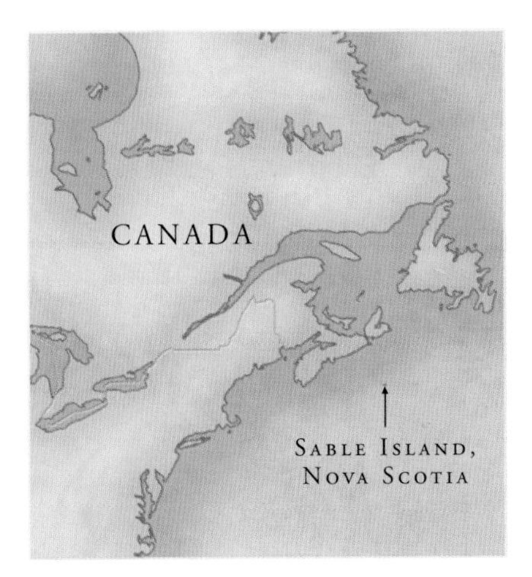

SABLE ISLAND *horse*

CANADA'S HORSE OF SAND AND SEA

According to folklore, the Sable Island horse originated from domestic horses that swam ashore from a ship that ran aground off the coast of the island. These horses gradually became adapted to the harsh conditions and established themselves on the island. In due course, they came to play a valuable role in the life-saving operations of the community.

A survivor

The Sable Island horse, which lives off the coast of Nova Scotia, shares similarities with other feral horses. Wild horses can be found all over the globe, and like this Canadian wild horse, some inhabit island homes. Like North Carolina's Banker horse (see pages 28–31) and Virginia's Chincoteague pony (see pages 32–37), the Sable Island horse forges its existence on a small spit of land. Also like its North American island cousins, it is feral, rather than wild, but unlike most other wild horses, which are governed, monitored, rounded up, and adopted out, the Sable Island horse is truly on its own.

There is no organization or agency to manage its population, grazing land or breeding numbers. Indeed, there has been no human interference since 1961, when the herd gained legal protection under the Sable Island Regulations of the Canada Shipping Act (see page 27). Therefore, these horses go it alone, forming their own bands, finding their own food and water, living or dying by the elements and predators, depending on no one.

LEFT *The Sable Island horses make their home near 'The Graveyard of the Atlantic,' where weather and the island have played a part in some 350 shipwrecks.*

A settlement horse

Sable Island isn't really an island at all. 'Sable' means 'sand' in French and this stretch of land is a sand bar, 42 km (26 miles) long and 1.5 km (1 mile) wide, off the coast of Nova Scotia.

There is probably little truth in the folklore about its origins. It is more likely to be derived from horses of the Acadians (French colonists). These horses were imported deliberately by Thomas Hancock, a Boston Massachusetts merchant, in 1760, as part of his unsuccessful attempt to start a farming settlement. The horses easily adapted to life in the wild, breaking up into small herds. Each herd had a range of about 3 km^2 (1.2 sq. miles, or 770 acres) and there were about 40 groups on the island.

Although the original shipwreck may be only legend, shipwrecks did play a genuine role in the horses' lives. Beginning in 1801, riding and draught horses were used on the island's life-saving stations to help the victims of shipwrecks. These stations operated well into the mid-1900s and, during this time, other breeds were introduced into the wild herds to improve the native stock.

Withstanding the elements

The Sable Island horses vary in size and conformation, like many American feral horses. Most are robust; close-coupled, stout horses designed for harsh conditions. They have medium-sized heads, some with straight profiles and others with convex profiles, that taper to small muzzles. They also have small ears, relatively short necks, deep chests, sturdy shoulders and short, straight legs with ample bone.

BELOW *Centuries of foraging in snow for dried grasses have given the Sable Island horse strong, flinty hooves.*

Life on a Canadian island

The climate on Sable Island is not as harsh as that on mainland Nova Scotia. While it receives more wind and fog, and the least amount of sunshine than anywhere else in Nova Scotia, it has milder temperatures. Winters are usually between +5°C (41°F) and –5°C (23°F), and seldom fall below –13°C (9°F). Summers peak in August at 25°C (77°F). Winter winds can reach up to 25 knots (about 50 km/h or 30 mph), but summer breezes can hit 10 knots (about 20 km/h or 11.5 mph).

When the island winters are mild, the numbers of horses increase, but when they are cruel and frigid, many of the older or weaker horses die, and the numbers fall. In 1960, the population of horses grew so large that the surplus horses were rounded up, shipped to the mainland and sold.

ABOVE *When herd numbers swell, environmentalists discuss the relocation of some horses off the island.*

BELOW *Mild summers provide the horses with ample pasture, in contrast to the winter snows.*

The Sable Island horses number between 200 and 350 at any given time. When the herds increase in size, environmentalists and others begin to disuss population control. They argue that the horses are becoming stunted due to inbreeding and lack of good forage. They say that relocation will benefit the horses because they are not native to the island, and claim that they have a negative impact on the ecosystem. However, there is no substantial evidence to back many of these claims.

Although access to the island is restricted – by its location and by regulations – the horses are of great interest, both culturally and scientifically.

The Sable Island horse today

Currently, the horses enjoy the protection of the Sable Island Regulations, but only as long as the horses and their island habitat are effectively monitored. Since 1801, when the life-saving stations were established, there has been a continuous government presence on Sable Island. The Canadian government is now debating whether to close the last remaining station, which would bring the human occupation of the island to an end – and puts into question the future of Sable Island. This option would place not only the horses but all the island's wildlife at serious risk.

Most of the work at the station involves weather-data collection and research, but the station also provides benefits to the island's infrastructure and security. These include the maintenance of navigation aids, wildlife research and support services to the offshore energy industry. A change of government could change all this and, in turn, change the future of the island's wildlife. For now, however, it is left to the horses.

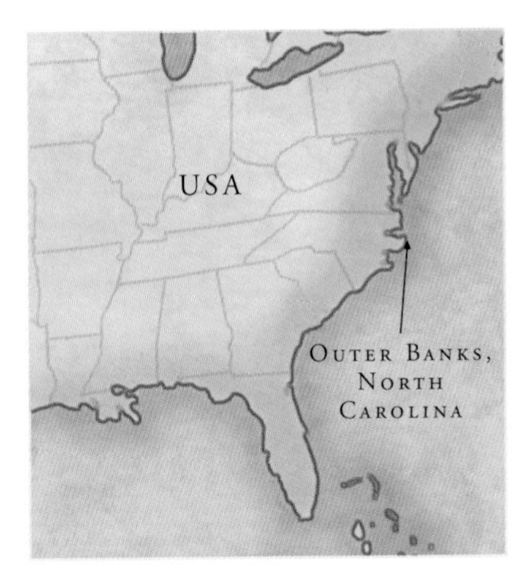

Banker *horse*

North Carolina's sand-bank horses

These small horses live on the Outer Banks, which are sand banks that appear and disappear with the ebb and flow of the tides. Subject to harsh weather, battered by often violent storms, surviving on scant forage during sweltering summers, and struggling against human interference, the Bankers continue to thrive, as they have for centuries.

Marsh tackies and sand ponies

The Outer Banks are a string of small islands within close range of the fashionable coastal resorts of North Carolina. It is from these that the Banker horse, or Banker, gets its name. The largest herd lives on Shackleford Island, where it is known as the Shackleford or Shackleford Banks pony. Other herds live on Ocracoke Island (the Ocracoke pony) and around the mainland town of Corolla (the Corolla pony). In earlier days, the residents of the islands referred to them as 'marsh tackies' or 'sand ponies'.

Spanish beginnings

Like many of North America's feral horses, the origins of the Banker horse lie with the Spanish explorers of the New World. In 1492, shortly after their arrival in the Antilles, specifically Hispaniola, these explorers set up breeding stations. Their horses served the mainland's needs for saddle horses and work horses. An exploration party of five hundred men, headed by Luis Vazquez de Ayllon, took nearly a hundred Spanish horses and headed up the

LEFT *The horses were a common sight in Colonial times and so became known as 'Tackies', from the British usage meaning 'common'.*

ABOVE *Bankers are genetically unique and, although small and hardy, deserve protection.*

coastline. The experience took its toll on the party: some reports say that many perished from disease while others point to battles with native tribes. Those who survived returned to Hispaniola but left their horses to fend for themselves. This scenario repeated itself a few years later, when they abandoned their horses rather than forcing them to make the journey home.

Forsaken, these tough little Spanish horses, for the most part, were better able to weather the conditions than their former carers. They found refuge on the Shackleford Banks, within a stone's throw of the coast. Decade by decade, their numbers grew but, because of their isolation, their bloodlines stayed pure. They were able to continue unabated, even through the 1800s when settlers moved into the area now known as North Carolina.

The horses continued to thrive, even through the 20th century. The new settlers, and other local communities, saw their potential and used them for transport, ploughing and pulling in fishing nets. An issue of *National Geographic Magazine* in 1926 included an article on motor-coaching through North Carolina, noting that between 5,000 and 6,000 wild horses roamed the sand banks of North Carolina. However, this situation was not to last.

Modern world, new challenges

With the increase in urbanization and the demand for land, the Banker horses were faced with a new challenge. Civilization was encroaching in the form of up-market resorts and condominiums, as the desirable coastal area was rapidly developed for the property market. Throughout the 1970s and 1980s, the sleepy seaside village of Corolla changed into an up-market holiday destination. Some horses were victims of this progress: a new highway was cut through the Outer Banks to ease traffic congestion and, during its inaugural year, seven horses died after being struck by vehicles.

Development in the area continued, and local residents and incoming tourists took over the land where the horses originally roamed. The wild horses were in the way. Some died in traffic accidents; others were shot. It was difficult to find a balance between development and cultural heritage.

Fortunately, concerned local individuals formed groups to protect the horses and move them to more remote locations. Herds were given protection on various islands. Currently, the new reserve which lies within the Currituck National Wildlife Refuge, although distant, gives the Corolla herd more safety. Other herds find refuge on outlying islands.

One such herd, of about a hundred horses, lives on Shackleford Island, off Beaufort, North Carolina. In 1996, these horses faced a grim future when 74 horses were destroyed after testing positive for equine infectious anaemia.

The National Park Service at Cape Lookout National Seashore, in cooperation with the Foundation for Shackleford Wild Horses, manages the

Shackleford herd. The Foundation has set up a studbook for establishing the Banker horse as a breed, which is registered with the American Livestock Breeds Conservancy. Birth control and adoption are two methods being used to maintain the Shackleford herd and its environment. Also, in 1989, the Corolla Wild Horse Fund was set up to raise public awareness.

Challenges continue to face the Banker horse, but now that it is considered to be a genetically unique equine, with a history worth preserving, it is beginning to receive the protection that it deserves.

A noble descent

As a breed, Bankers are remarkable for being feral, yet pure of blood. Research into its bloodlines proves that it is not only of Iberian descent but also belongs to a group of genetically pure horses, such as the Paso Fino and the Pryor Mountain horse (see pages 62–65), which were proven to contain pure Spanish blood.

The Banker horse is often pony-sized but is still proportioned like a horse. It is close-coupled and compact, with an upright neck, a long shoulder, an ample-sized head and straight profile. Its legs are slender but strong, with tough feet, which are ideal for pawing the sand to reveal fresh drinking water. The horse bears a full mane and a full, well-set tail. Most are buckskin, dun, bay, chestnut and brown in colour and, in the Shackleford herd, there are even some pinto colorations.

An interesting characteristic of the Banker horse is that many, like their Spanish Paso brothers, are gaited. Renowned geneticist Dr D. Phillip Sponenberg noted that the horse can possess a variety of gaits, including the running walk, single-foot, amble, pace and some Paso gaits. These gaits are inherited – not taught.

BELOW *The Banker horse is able to find nutrition in the salty marsh grasses of the islands.*

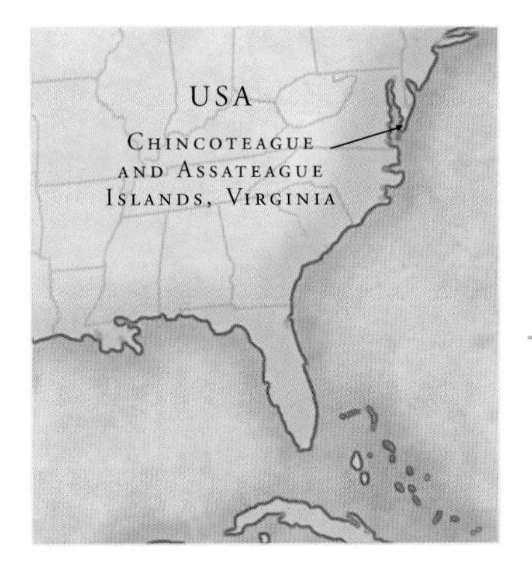

Chincoteague *pony*

Virginia's fairy-tale island pony

The Assateague and Chincoteague islands, located just on the sea side of Chesapeake Bay, Virginia, have been home to feral ponies since the 1700s. Small and hardy, these ponies have prospered despite the extreme weather and limited forage, relying on the cord grass of the saltmarsh and the seaweeds that are indigenous to these wind-whipped islands.

Into the melting pot

For the most part, feral Chincoteague ponies breed through the process of natural selection. There is considerable variation in their breed characteristics, and all kinds of conformation, colour and bloodlines are evident. There are signs of Welsh, Arabian and mustang influence since these horses were put in to breed with the original feral herds.

Chincoteague ponies generally have a petite profile with wide-set eyes and a broad forehead. Some have Arabian-like dished faces, but occasionally their mustang blood will come through and give a more straight profile. They usually have short, close-coupled bodies, with good sloping shoulders and round hindquarters. Their legs have good solid bone and tough hooves.

Because of their mixed breeding, they can be any size from 12 to 14 hands (122–147.5 cm/48–58 in), or taller. While pinto markings, made famous by Misty's 'map of America' (see page 34), are common, you will find ponies in nearly every coat colour.

LEFT *Chincoteague ponies are commonly piebald or skewbald. In America this is known as pinto colouring.*

ABOVE *Mares in foal give birth on the island in early to late spring.*

Magical 'Misty'

In 1947, Marguerite Henry's book *Misty of Chincoteague* hit the bookshops. This tale traced the fanciful origins of the Chincoteague pony and followed the life of the Beebe children, the wild pony mare Phantom, and her spirited, quizzical foal Misty. An award-winning classic, it is still enjoyed today by American children. Misty had pinto markings on her side, which resembled a map of America, and a blaze, which was shaped like the state of Virginia.

Early island home

According to legend, during the 16th century, a Spanish galleon carrying horses to the New World was wrecked while coming ashore, and the horses fell overboard, many swimming to the safety of Assateague Island. Some French enthusiasts of the Pottok pony go a step further, surmising that the ponies of Assateague, often coloured, could be related to the Pottok, which was scheduled for import by Spanish explorers during the 16th and 17th centuries, as a pack horse for the New World.

While this is the most romantic notion of how the ponies came into being, other theories, a little more based in reality, are probably more accurate. The horses were probably released into the wilds of Assateague in the 17th century by Virginia settlers who wished to avoid being taxed on their livestock. Alternatively, they may have been the property of colonists who did not have properly fenced farms and who wanted to make sure their horses did not escape into the Virginia hills. The horses were soon joined by other livestock, including cattle, sheep and hogs.

Pony-penning

In the 1700s, farmers decided to round up the horses in order to work their land. They wanted to lay claim to the ponies quickly, so they put aside a day to 'pen' the wild ponies, herding them up, then branding them and breaking them for work. This became a regular occasion and, by the late 18th century, the penning of both ponies and sheep had became an annual event.

The early days

In the 1800s, the round-up became more popular among island residents. The whole community on Chincoteague anticipated the day and the penning turned into a festival. The event became something of a tourist attraction, which was a boon for local businesses. In 1909, it was decided to set aside an annual date, and so the last Wednesday and Thursday of July became official pony-penning days. Sheep-penning, however, did not fare as well in the hearts of locals and came to an end in 1914.

With general tourism boosting the island's commerce all-year round, it became important to safeguard the well-being of visitors. After two tragic fires struck the islands in the 1920s, the Chincoteague Volunteer Fire Department (CVFD) was founded. The volunteers had the manpower, but still needed a way to keep this young department financially afloat. The answer was to take the money raised at pony-penning and its accompanying carnival and use it to purchase equipment and supplies for the fire department. The department in turn would be responsible for caring for the herd and overseeing the penning.

In the 1920s, Samuel Fields, a wealthy farmer, bought up a huge portion of Assateague – particularly at the southern end, which was known to be full of oysters. This forced many villagers to move to Chincoteague. It also changed the structure of pony-penning and, in 1923, the event was moved

BELOW *Most visitors to Assateague are eager to see one of the spotted ponies that the island is so famous for.*

ABOVE *Life on the windswept island of Assateague is often challenging.*

to its permanent home on Chincoteague. The pony herds were initially transferred by boat until, in 1925, they were made to swim across the narrow, shallow channel – and thus the modern era of pony-penning began. Tourists soon heard of the amazing swimming ponies and began to arrive from all over the country for the annual penning. By the next decade, nearly 25,000 tourists and residents were turning up to witness this event.

Firemen to the rescue

The CVFD took its new role as caretaker of the wild ponies seriously and began to monitor their health and well-being. One area which particularly concerned them was the limited gene pool, since no new horses had been introduced to the herd for generations. In 1939, the CVFD set 20 mustangs free on the island to breed with the ponies. Some years later, Arabian stock was also introduced to help bring back the herd's refined features, which had been diluted by the mustang blood.

In 1943, Assateague Island was purchased by the federal government and divided into the Assateague National Seashore Park and the Chincoteague National Wildlife Refuge. The CVFD continued its job of caring for the ponies and continued to hold its annual pony-penning event. With all the money that came in from pony-penning days, the CVFD was able to completely upgrade its equipment and facilities. In 1947, coinciding with the publication of *Misty of Chincoteague*, the department sought out ponies that were locally owned, purchased them and began their own fire department herd, which they moved to Assateague. After this time, the government no longer allowed local residents to graze their herds on Assateague, reserving that privilege for these publicly owned feral herds.

Pony-penning today

Chincoteague Island has become a tourist attraction for horse-lovers around the world, who visit annually during July. To this day, the penning and festival are this area's biggest attractions. The CVFD's Carnival starts well in advance, but the big days are in the final week. Thursday morning is the day of the swim. The start time is flexible because the event organizers want to ensure the safety of the ponies and need to take factors such as tide, currents and the readiness of the ponies into consideration.

Local ranchers and riders become 'saltwater cowboys' during the event, as they gather up the ponies and herd them to the shore for the swim. This takes place across the narrowest part of the Assateague Channel at low tide, beginning at Chincoteague Memorial Park on the eastern side of the island.

On their arrival on Chincoteague, the ponies are given a rest and a full examination by veterinarians to make sure that they suffered no ill-effects from the swim. Soon after, they make their way through the town by trotting down roads that lead to a corral at the Carnival grounds, where they stay until the next day's auction.

The auction is the part that everyone waits for, but people also enjoy themselves by having a bite to eat in the dining room at the Carnival grounds, served by the Ladies' Auxiliary, just as they have done for decades. The fairground rides and games also help to keep visitors in high spirits, and live music and a raffle round out the Carnival's events. On Friday the horses that were not sold in the auction swim back to Assateague for another year of living free.

Interest in the ponies has increased in the last couple of decades and, because not everyone can make it to Virginia to buy a pony, Chincoteague lovers are starting up their own breeding operations, creating domestic herds of Chincoteague ponies from once feral ponies. This has opened up a new world of opportunity for the Chincoteague pony, and as a result, it can now be found all over North America.

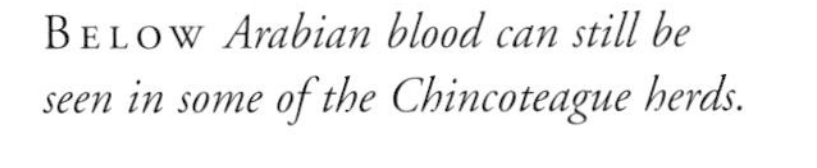

BELOW *Arabian blood can still be seen in some of the Chincoteague herds.*

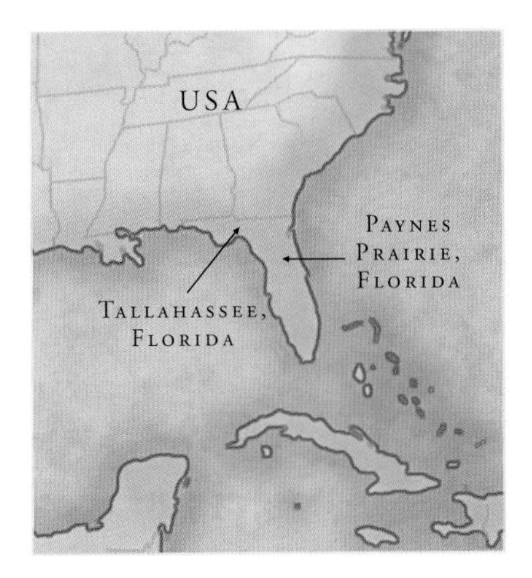

FLORIDA CRACKER *horse*

LITTLE COWHORSE OF AMERICA'S SOUTH

The modern Cracker horse is thought to owe its existence to the Spanish explorer Ponce de León, who originally set out in 1513 to search for an imaginary land called the Fountain of Youth. He failed to find it but, instead, became the first European to set foot in what he christened La Florida, meaning 'flowery'.

Spanish origins

In 1521, on his second expedition to what is now known as Florida, de León brought 200 men and much-needed supplies, including horses and cattle. As the colonists set up breeding stations, further expeditions brought even more Spanish horses. As the herds grew, some horses were set loose, others were left to wander away when their owners returned to Spain, and a few escaped.

These horses actually had their origins a little further south than Spain: in North Africa. The Barb horses were very influential on these Iberian mounts. Genetic similarities to these horses are found throughout the region, due to the number of breeding stations set up by the Spanish and the types of horses they bred. Like the Peruvian Paso, the Paso Fino and the Criollo (see pages 76–79), the horses of Florida had Spanish Barb and other horses, such as the Sorraia (see pages 128–133), the gaited Spanish Jennet and the Andalusian.

A Native American connection

LEFT *The Cracker has an alert expression, with keen, wide-set eyes, a straight profile, and tapering muzzle.*

Small bands of wild horses were scattered all over the American South and, as different horses joined the herds, each breed introduced some new traits.

ABOVE *Reserves within Florida are helping the herd numbers improve.*

Wandering herds were a common sight until Florida became a possession of the USA in 1821.

Native American tribes – particularly the Seminole – found the horses to be a rich resource and captured and trained them for riding. The horses, now acclimatized to the humid summers and often torrential thunderstorms, were able to perform well in their environment, so much so that when the Spanish settlers of the 1700s found them, they also started to use them.

When ranchers set up their cattle operations in the lush flatlands of Florida, the horses of Spanish descent readily took to their role as cattle horses. As agriculture became a bigger enterprise, the horses played an even more vital role on the sprawling ranchland.

Cattle were driven and herded with these small, hardy horses. The Spanish cattlemen did not use lariats to keep their herds in check; instead, they carried long bullwhips, which would sing with loud cracks as the cowboys snapped them. The horses, with their steady nature, learned to be unaffected by this constant noise going on above their heads. Both the cattlemen and their horses became known as 'Crackers'. This was not the horses' only name; they were also called Seminole ponies, Prairie ponies and Florida cow ponies.

Good cow sense

The Cracker horses had an innate cow-herding sense and were extremely quick on their feet and agile, capable of matching an errant cow's every move. They also possessed immense stamina – a byproduct of both their genetics and their adaptation to their new home. Cowboys particularly liked the Crackers because many of them possessed a smooth unique gait, called the 'coon rack'. This ambling single-foot gait gave a comfortable ride and was easy on the horse, rather than the strain of trotting or cantering all day.

At the turn of the 20th century, the once-flourishing numbers of Cracker horses, like those of other horses replaced by mechanization, suddenly took a downward turn, but for different reasons: rather than being replaced by tractors, their work disappeared, or rather, relocated. The Midwestern cattle ranches of the Depression Era were hit doubly hard by record drought. Once lush pasture turned into barren plain, which became known as the Dust Bowl, and ranchers desperate to keep afloat took government assistance and moved their operations to better lands – in this case, Florida.

These new cattle, however, introduced an internal parasite to the state: the screw-worm. In itself, this was not a major disaster, but the cows did need to be treated with a deworming medication. And while the nimble little Cracker horse was fine for herding cattle, it was no match for an angry cow in distress at being roped and held down for the purpose of drug administration. Instead, the Quarter horse, a larger, powerful horse with English Thoroughbred origins, became the cow horse of choice. The Cracker's reign as a cowboy's mount was over. Breeding slowed and the numbers of horses began to dwindle.

The Cracker today

Not everyone lost interest in the Cracker, however. Several ranching families kept their breeding operations intact. The Ayers, Bronson, Harvey, Matchetts, Partin and Whaley families were major contributors to the preservation of the modern Cracker horse.

Several reserves within the state of Florida sprang up in the late 1900s. In 1984, John Ayers, a member of one of the original families, gave a small herd to Florida's Department of Agriculture and Consumer Services. This was placed within the Withlacoochee State Forest and Florida Agricultural Museum in Tallahassee. The next year, Ayers also sold six mares to the Friends of the Paynes Prairie, where they were released on to the 85 km^2 (33 sq. miles) of the Paynes Prairie State Preserve, an original home to thousands of Crackers. On these reserves they live as they did for hundreds of years previously.

An association was founded to preserve and protect the breed, registering horses under strict guidelines. Today, thanks to the efforts of the Florida Cracker Horse Association, the number of horses registered is nearly a thousand. As members of the public become more aware of the existence of the horse, they understand that this breed is part of the Sunshine State's history and needs to be preserved for the future.

BELOW *Despite its small size, the Cracker appears more like a horse than a pony.*

Small but hardy

The Cracker is, on average, the size of a pony, ranging from 13.2 hands (137 cm/54 in) up to no more than 15 hands (152 cm/60 in) in height. However, it has horse-like rather than pony-like characteristics: a pretty head with a fine muzzle, wide-set eyes and an intelligent face. It has a well-formed neck and clean throatlatch, a short back, an ample ribcage and a nicely sloping croup. The slender legs contribute to the overall light-boned appearance and the tail is medium set.

ABACO BARB

THE RAREST HORSE OF THE BAHAMAS – AND THE WORLD

Often referred to as the breed of horse closest to extinction, the Abaco Barb remains a fragile branch on the Spanish Barb's family tree. On the Bahamian island of Great Abaco, some 320 km (200 miles) off the coast of Florida, fewer than 15 horses remain from a once robust herd of 200, and the breed is now critically endangered.

Life in the Caribbean

This small tribe of feral horses can trace its history back several hundred years to the time of the Spanish exploration of the New World. In the Caribbean, Spanish colonists set up areas specifically for horse-breeding and produced cavalry horses, work horses and saddle horses. These animals were then shipped from the islands to North and South America. Some 13 ships never reached their destination and were wrecked around the Abaco Islands.

Many of the horses on these shipwrecked vessels swam to the safety of Abaco's shores. Great Abaco Island has naturally protected waters and dozens of offshore cays covering more than 209 km^2 (130 sq m) of azure coastline. This island, where lush pine forests provided protection from the often-violent tropical storms, proved to be an ideal home for the animals. They could forage for sustenance easily among the trees and gallop away along the white sandy shores if danger loomed. Centuries went by and these shipwrecked Spanish horses enjoyed a problem-free feral life. Without human intervention, the herd's bloodlines remained pure and the numbers grew to a healthy 200.

LEFT *Only a handful of these horses remain on the island of Great Abaco.*

ABOVE *The remaining Abaco horses live on a preserve in the pine forests of Great Abaco, their traditional habitat.*

An uneasy alliance

All this changed in the 20th century when the first people set up home on the island and it was no longer just for wildlife. The settlers began to take advantage of all the natural resources of Great Abaco, including the opportunity to hunt. Wild boar were plentiful, and the hunters relished the abundant game. A paved road was carved through the island to make it easier for the new settlers to get from one side of the island to the other. Sadly, the horses also suffered at the hands of the hunters because their dogs often pursued the horses instead of boar.

The horses suffered a further blow after an innocent, but tragic event. In the 1960s, a child climbed on to a wild horse, and the horse reacted like any other untamed creature: it bolted and the child was killed. Vengeance was swift: the villagers slaughtered all but three of the island's horses.

Some Abaco residents intervened and took the surviving horses to an area of the island called Treasure Cay and, within three decades, the horses had bred to a small band of 35. In the early 1990s, however, that number was cut by half, partly due to the poor foresight of the islanders. Horses died from lack of medical attention, from pesticide poisoning and even from mortal wounds inflicted by dogs and people. No foals have been born since 1998, although a couple of mares have been in foal. In 2004, only a dozen horses were counted on Great Abaco island and it was realized that these horses were critically in danger of disappearing from the planet forever.

The Abaco today

In 2002, after 10 years of extensive research into its bloodlines, it was determined that the Abaco was a strain of the Spanish Barb horses, dating back to the original stock brought over from the Barbary Coast of North Africa by the Spanish colonists. This was backed by DNA evidence, and the horses, now known as Abaco Barbs – perhaps the purest strain in existence – were brought into the Horses of the Americas registry.

With support from the government of the Bahamas, a reserve has now been set aside so that the animals can live once again in their original habitat. Due to their precarious situation, however, no Abaco Barbs on the island can ever be sold, but instead will be protected on their reserve.

Concerned individuals continue to come to the aid of the Abaco. The Wild Horses of Abaco Preservation Society (WHOA) has worked since 1992 to save the remaining horses and to publicize their predicament. In addition, Milanne Rehor, the founder of the Abaco Wild Horse Fund has worked constantly to get the Bahamian government to see that the Abaco horses need continual protection.

BELOW *This pinto barb bears a rare 'medicine hat' marking: colour on the ears and head, surrounded by white.*

Descendants of the Spanish Barb

Like their Barb brothers, the Abaco wild horses are small, sturdy and compact animals, with light but extremely strong bones in the legs. Pesticide poisoning and rich feed from their days at Treasure Cay have weakened the once tough hooves, but the surviving horses remain nimble and sure-footed. Many of the horses bear splashes – white patches, usually along the lower half of the body – which are characteristic of the true Spanish Barb. They also sport thick manes and full tails, and have a great deal of stamina and endurance.

AMERICAN *mustang*

HERITAGE OF THE AMERICAN WEST

Although evidence shows that horses roamed North America 10,000 years ago, for reasons unknown, they vanished from the landscape until the Spanish conquistadors arrived in the 16th century. The Iberian horses that they brought with them were of Barb blood – descendants of the horses that accompanied the North African Berbers during their invasion of Spain in the 8th century.

A break for freedom

Being on horseback enabled the Spanish explorers to conquer the indigenous people and they then set up breeding facilities near Santa Fé, New Mexico. However, not everyone respected the new conquerors and their ways. Many Native American tribes, particularly the Apache, 'liberated' dozens of these horses and brought them deeper into North America.

A few horses escaped or wandered off and began a new life of freedom. They took to the open plains, to the foothills and to the mountains. Those that survived the winters passed their genes on to new generations.

The product of a harsh environment

LEFT *The US government decides how many mustangs can live on public lands.*

While many picture mustangs with rippling coats and long, waving manes and tails, this is not always entirely accurate. The mustang has adapted to its environment and, as a result, is not always the prettiest of horses.

ABOVE *Roundups, which used to take place on horseback, are now controlled and managed from the air.*

Mustangs come in various shapes and sizes, but they usually have short legs, short necks and large heads, often with Roman noses. Their coats, which are of all colours and patterns, are often scarred as a result of living in inhospitable conditions. Although they are usually pony-sized, some may be up to 15 hands (152.5 cm/60 in).

The new frontier

By the 19th century, these now feral horses had became more cunning, hardy and enduring, and had expanded throughout the untamed West. They had became known as mustangs, an Americanization of the Spanish word *mesteño*, meaning 'wild', or 'ownerless'.

However, the American West did not remain virgin territory for long: American ranchers and settlers headed away from the big cities east of the Mississippi River, seeking to start a new life. In the early 1900s, cattle-ranching operations vied with the mustangs for grazing space on public lands. The West was no longer a frontier – it was settled. Once the petrol engine was invented, the fate of the working horse was sealed.

And as for the wild horse? It was a nuisance for the ranchers who leased public lands from the government. So began the mustang slaughter. Hundreds of thousands of horses were captured and shot, and their bodies ground into pet food. At the beginning of the 20th century, more than 2 million wild horses roamed the West; by 1926 the number had declined to half this figure.

The fight to save the mustang

Throughout the 1950s, individuals tried to protest about the mass destruction of the mustang. Velma Johnson, nicknamed 'Wild Horse Annie' by her detractors, fought to get newspapers and television interested in the plight of the wild horses.

Johnson helped to convince the US government that the wholesale slaughter of wild horses and burros, which had continued unchecked since the 1930s, was unacceptable to the American people. In 1959, the hunting of wild horses by plane was banned.

Legal protection

In 1960, the International Society for the Protection of Mustangs and Burros was formed to create legislation to save the mustang from being wiped out.

Next, in 1971, the US Congress passed the Wild Free-Roaming Horse and Burro Act to stop the abuse and exploitation of the mustangs, stating that they were 'living symbols of the historic and pioneer spirit of the West, they contribute to the diversity of life forms within the nation'. The Bureau of Land Management (BLM) was put in charge of protecting the horses and enforcing the new laws.

According to these laws, it was prohibited to remove mustangs from publicly owned land, to shoot them on public lands, to exploit them for commercial purposes and, in the case of private parties, to take them without permission. However, many of these activities continued to take place.

Adoption scheme

In 1976, the BLM introduced its Adopt-A-Horse programme, allowing people to buy a mustang for a small fee. The horse remained the property of the government for a year, then the adopter was given full ownership. Over the years, the BLM has had other challenges to face in its management of the mustangs. Historically, it has bowed to pressure from ranchers, who graze more than 4 million cattle on public lands. Today there are an estimated 250 cattle to every wild horse or burro on public land.

The mustang today

Mustang numbers are now estimated at 37,000 by the BLM and 26,000 by the American Mustang and Burro Association and other advocacy groups. They roam freely in 11 states; the largest numbers (Comstock wild horses, see pages 50–53) are found in Nevada, and the second largest (Pryor Mountain horses, see pages 62–65), are found in Wyoming. They are also found in Washington, Oregon (Kiger mustangs, see pages 70–73), Idaho, Utah (Sulphur Springs mustangs, see pages 54–57), Colorado, Montana, and California (Coyote Canyon horses, see pages 58–61). One band is left in Arizona, a few remain in New Mexico, and a few hundred free-roaming horses survive in Alberta and British Columbia.

BELOW *In 1971, there were 303 mustang herd management areas; today there are 201.*

Their habitats are dwindling, and the BLM has claimed that their ever-increasing numbers have led to a surplus of horses. Conditions on the ranges have not improved, and the Adopt-a-Horse programme has reached its limit.

In January 2005, a polemic amendment known as the 'Burns rider' was attached to an appropriations bill. The US Congress modified the adoption programme to allow the sale (the result usually being slaughter) of captured horses that are 'more than 10 years of age' or have been 'offered unsuccessfully for adoption at least three times'. Due to the controversy provoked, there is a movement to have it repealed and the original wording restored.

Animal welfare organizations continue to be the watchdogs for the treatment of mustangs, while mustang associations aim to increase awareness and educate adopters and the public.

COMSTOCK *wild horse*

MUSTANGS OF THE GOLD-RUSH ERA

The Comstock horse has a unique history that parallels the silver and gold rushes of the mid-1800s. The prospectors who flooded into Nevada brought their own horses to work in the mines but set them loose when they were no longer needed. It is from these and other abandoned domestic horses that the Comstock is descended.

A mining background

The discovery of silver, and then gold, in the 1800s, brought a flood of prospectors into Nevada, and the silver mines that operated throughout the 19th century turned Virginia City into both a boomtown and the capital of Nevada. Horses were used in the mines to carry out and transport the heavy silver, and also on the expanding cattle ranches. During the gold rush, the prospectors worked at fever pitch, seeking their fortunes. If they did not strike it lucky in Virginia City, they simply packed up and moved on to San Francisco, leaving their horses behind. Horses that were no longer needed in the mines or for the wagon trains, or whose owners who could no longer afford to feed them, were also turned loose and left to fend for themselves.

As Virginia City is situated at 1,435 m (4,700 ft) in the Sierra Nevada, it does not suffer from extreme desert conditions or ferocious heat. As a result, the abandoned horses formed bands and did well on their own, their numbers growing from a few dozen to more than a thousand. However, a population of now-wild horses was not popular by local people. The horses were left alone until recently, when their management became inevitable.

LEFT *The Nevada Department of Agriculture, which has authority over the Comstock wild horse, refers to them as 'feral' or 'estray'.*

ABOVE *Some Comstock horses roam into areas that are inhabited by humans.*

Suburban challenges

Unlike the mustangs that live on publicly owned lands and are managed by the Bureau of Land Management (BLM), the free-roaming Comstock horses live on private property and therefore do not come under the jurisdiction of the US federal government. Consequently, they are not protected by the 1971 Wild Free-Roaming Horse and Burro Act because they are not classed as 'wild' by the government.

Like other mustangs, the Comstock horse has had its challenges, particularly in modern times. In the last two decades, with the explosion in Nevada's human population, sprawling suburbs have developed, and as a result the horses have lost much of their habitat. They are being forced higher into the mountains, where food is more scarce, and have begun to wander into the suburbs in search of food. As the numbers of residents increase, so do the hazards of living in close proximity to people, and many horses have been killed or left to die after collisions with vehicles.

One of the most gruesome clashes with people occurred in 1998, when three young men decided that the horses would make good target practice and shot 33 of them dead. The story reached the national news and, as a result, a number of groups formed to publicize the plight of the horses.

The Nevada Department of Agriculture began to trap horses that were becoming too familiar in neighbourhoods or a nuisance to people and traffic, and offer them for adoption through private groups, any unadopted horses being sent to auction. Four wild horse groups – the Least Resistant Training Concepts (LRTC), the Virginia Range Wildlife Protection Association, Mustang-Spirit and Lifesavers Wild Horse Rescue – have got together and removed as many horses as they could from the state holding facility.

Another group, the Let 'em Run Foundation, works with other groups to set aside land for a sanctuary, so that visitors can observe the wild horses in a natural setting and see how the herd is managed (and witness their training, which is aimed at making the horses more suitable for adoption).

A shy horse

Comstock horses, like other mustangs, are variable in size, but generally on the small side. They come in all coat patterns, although most are bay or sorrel. Most are shy, although with increasing urbanization and shortage of food, they are becoming bolder around people.

BELOW *Horses that are trapped by the Nevada government are placed in a state holding facility for adoption.*

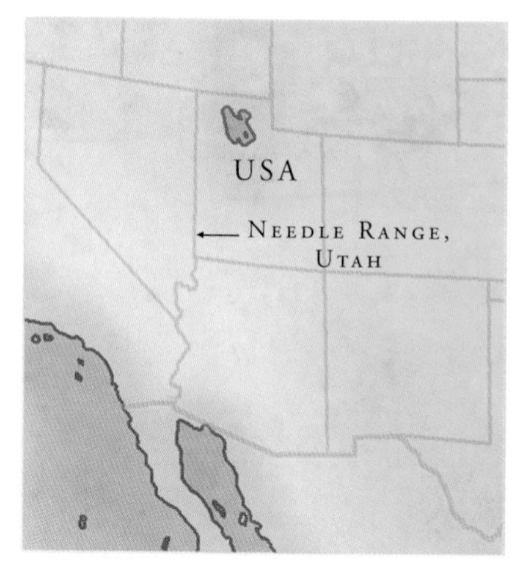

Sulphur Springs *mustang*

Of Spanish blood

Few modern-day mustangs carry the genes of Spanish horses, since so many other breeds and types of horses have been introduced over the decades. But there are cases where isolated herds, left alone and without human influence, have retained Spanish blood. The Sulphur Springs mustang is one such case.

True to type

In the 11 American states where the Bureau of Land Management (BLM) manages horses, there are 201 herd areas. In Utah, about 3,600 horses are found, in 23 different herds, throughout the state. The Needle Range of mountains, in south-western Utah state, has a herd that remains true to its Spanish origins. These are known as the Sulphur Springs mustangs, or sometimes the Spanish Sulphur. Geneticists have found these horses to be one of the purest Spanish herds left in the wild. Like other horses on public land, they are managed by the BLM.

The Old Spanish Trail

When Spain still occupied the western territories of North America, the Old Spanish Trail, a well-worn path over mountain and desert, linked El Pueblo de Nuestra Señora la Reina de Los Ángeles de Porciúncula (or Los Angeles), in California, to the Villa Real de la Santa Fé de San Francisco de Asísi (or Santa Fé), in New Mexico. This route allowed traders to bring blankets from

LEFT *The Sulphur Springs herd is genetically unique, and so gains special attention from the US government.*

New Mexico and furs from Utah into the southern California valley, where they were traded for Spanish horses and mules. This trail was a haven for thieves, who often stole horses along the way. In one major raid, thieves stole 3,000 head of horses from the Spanish missions in California and drove them over the Old Spanish Trail to Utah. It is these horses that are thought to be the forebears of the Sulphur mustangs.

Over time, the Sulphur herd bred with escaped ranch livestock, yet most retained many of their Spanish Barb traits and found refuge in the Utah mountains. Roaming an expansive, remote area of high desert basins and expansive mountain ranges, the mustangs flourished in the Needle Range. This austere, striking mountain range lies about 70 km (45 miles) west of Milford, Utah, near the Nevada border and in some areas rises to nearly 3,000 m (10,000 ft). From north to south, the mountainous spine of the Needle Range consists of two main peaks: Mountain Home Peak and Indian Peak.

BELOW *New DNA testing has confirmed that Sulphur Springs mustangs are closely related to Sorraia.*

Utah's zebra horses

The Sulphur Springs mustangs are pretty horses, usually dun, buckskin, grulla (mouse-grey) or red dun in colour. Other colours, found throughout the region, include bay, black, sorrel, palomino and roan. They have a dorsal stripe along the back, a bi-coloured mane and tail, tiger stripes on the legs and some chest bar lines.

The original Colonial Spanish horse displayed some characteristics of the extinct wild tarpan, and the Sulphur Springs mustangs also exhibit many of these primitive traits. These strong primitive markings have earned the herd the nickname 'Utah's Zebra Horses'.

Compact and small, and at about 14.2 hands (147.5 cm/58 in), these horses are thrifty and are able to survive on little feed. Very agile and possessing tremendous endurance, they have sloping croups, low-set tails, deep bodies and narrow chests, as well as broad foreheads, refined faces and neat muzzles, slender necks and ears curved at the tip.

Genetic testing

In the late 1990s and early 2000s, researchers and geneticists wanted to confirm that the Sulphur Springs mustangs were indeed one of the purest herds of Spanish horses left in the USA. The Sulphur herd has many of the physical traits of the Iberian Sorraia (see pages 128–133), which is the primitive ancestor of the Iberian native horses, and the scientists wanted to see if there was more than just a physical connection. German author Hardy Oelke conducted extensive research into these horses, including DNA tests, which showed a link between the Iberian Sorraia and the Sorraia mustangs of North America.

So far, research conducted on these horses has confirmed that they are indeed of Spanish descent. Dr Gus Cothran, director of the Equine Blood

ABOVE *Sulphur Springs horses are more uniform in colour and size than other mustang herds.*

Typing Research Laboratory at the University of Kentucky, tested blood samples from the herd and concluded that: 'the Sulphur herd in general appears to have strong Spanish links'.

The BLM currently manages the Sulphur herd, and one of its objectives is to increase the number of horses displaying the good conformation, colour or characteristics of the original Colonial Spanish type of horse. It wants to keep the current wild horse population as pure as possible with no introduction of outside animals into the herd area. It also strives to maintain a herd size of 135–180 head of adult horses above 2 years of age.

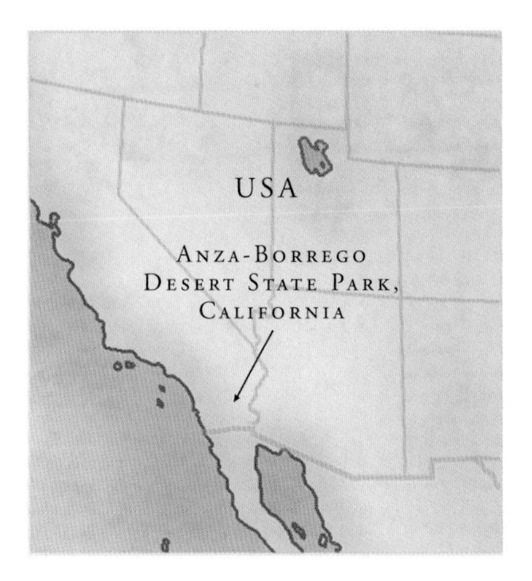

Coyote Canyon *horse*

Southern California's last mustang

Among the stretches of sand, large rocky outcrops and native chaparral of the Anza-Borrego Desert, wildlife still manages to exist. It is here, with the desert roadrunner, mountain lion, coyote and rattlesnake, that a small band of feral horses makes it home. These are the Coyote Canyon horses, the last remaining herd of wild horses in southern California.

Variation in the herd

Like other feral mustangs, the Coyote Canyon horse does not have a set 'breed standard' but shows some variation within the herd. Most of them are small, standing at no more than 14.5 hands (150 cm/59 in). Many have short, upright necks resting upon relatively well-sloped shoulders, short backs and powerful hindquarters. Their legs are on the short side but with strong bone and tough hoof horn. The head can be rather prominent, with large ears and large eyes.

Desert-dwellers

The desert area around Anza Borrego, to the north of California's San Diego, is renowned for its off-road vehicle trails, which allow visitors to explore the most inhospitable areas – as long as they have a sturdy four-wheel drive and good navigating skills!

LEFT *The displaced Coyote Canyon horses will most likely never be allowed back to their original homes.*

It is hard to pinpoint when these horses first came to the Anza-Borrego Desert, but they may have been introduced in about 1851, during a battle between Native American tribes. Alternatively, they may have been introduced earlier, when Spaniards, led by Pedro Fages, swept through the canyon in 1772, looking for deserters. Their horses could have either escaped or been traded with the local Cahuilla Indians. DNA testing of the Coyote Canyon horses has showed that, like many mustang herds, they have the blood of Spanish horses.

For a century, these horses have lived alongside the other wild creatures in this colourful desert. However, in March 2003, the remaining 29 horses were removed from their 4,000-hectare (100,000-acre) habitat in the Anza-Borrego Desert State park by the California State Parks government agency. A severe drought in the area, coupled with the threat of West Nile Virus, were the deciding factors in moving the horses towards water and better grazing. Another reason was the belief that the feral horses were competing with bighorn sheep for food and water, although studies proved that this was not the case.

RIGHT *Lack of water was a reason for the horses' removal, but no other animals were taken from the park.*

Government clashes

However, the Bureau of Land Management, a federal government agency, was charged with the care of these horses, not the state government, so they in fact had been illegally removed according to the Wild Free-Roaming Horse and Burro Act of 1971.

Senator Bill Morrow and co-sponsor Senator Dennis Hollingsworth introduced a bill to return the horses to Anza Borrego. It was argued that the herd had remained stable and survived several droughts, like the mustangs in Nevada, Arizona and other western states. More than a third of the herd was

25 years or older. So, because of all the politics, special interest groups and bureaucracy, the horses remain in limbo, even these many years later. In spite of their century of history in this desert, with everyone from cattle-ranchers to environmentalists contributing an opinion on their fate, the 29 horses will unfortunately probably meet the same demise as Morrow's bill, which never got out of committee.

If the federal government accepts the nomination of the Coyote Canyon Wild Horse Herd Historic District, it will be a milestone in the quest to preserve the mustangs, changing the terms of a fight repeating itself all over the West, where the wild horse's options are slowly disappearing.

BELOW *The US government stated that the herd was from horses abandoned in the 1930s, but bloodlines show Spanish mustang in their past.*

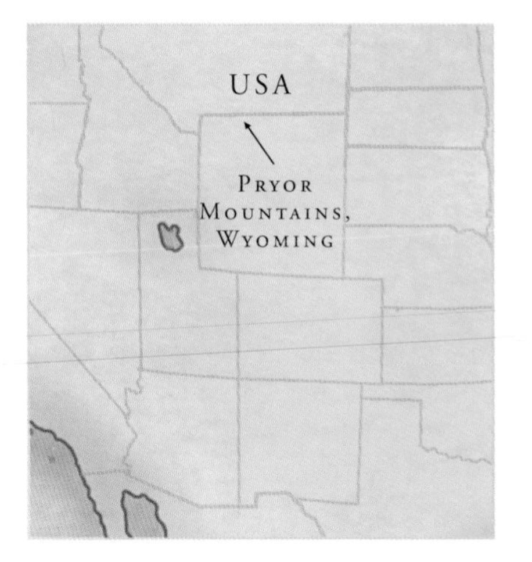

Pryor Mountain *horse*

Unique mustang of Wyoming

The herd of feral horses that has been living for nearly two centuries just outside of Lovell, Wyoming, is known as the Pryor Mountain mustangs. These small but hardy horses have adapted well to living in the mountainous and often-extreme terrain, where some of the highest peaks rise up to 2,650 m (8,700 ft) above sea level.

An ideal homeland

At higher altitudes in the Pryor Mountains, where the annual rainfall reaches 500 mm (20 in) or more, there is abundant grazing. The foothills, however, are dry, with scant scrub grass and sparse shrubs, and the arid red desert below this receives only 127–152 mm (5–6 in) of rainfall each year. It is the remoteness of this location that has protected the horses, leaving them true to type.

Although they currently number less than 200, because of their isolation they are excellent examples of horses of Spanish Colonial descent. Indeed, genetic testing of the horses by the Veterinary and Genetics Department of the University of Kentucky has verified that the horses have Colonial Spanish blood.

Mustangs of the north

LEFT *A battle-scarred stallion leaves a stud pile to mark his territory.*

There seems to be no doubt that the Pryor Mountain horses are directly descended from the conquistadors' Colonial Spanish horses. It is believed

ABOVE *Primitive markings such as leg stripes and dorsal stripes are a sign of ancient blood.*

that, while most mustangs are found in the south-west, these horses found their way north, possibly traded with the Crow tribe. Other people suggest that they are the descendants of escapes from the Lewis and Clark expedition of 1804–1806 – the first American overland expedition to the Pacific Coast and back – although this second scenario is less likely, given the fact that the expedition would have noticed if more than a couple of horses went missing.

September 1968 marked the creation of the Wild Horse Refuge in the Pryor Mountains. Through the diligent efforts of the Pryor Mountain Wild Horse Association of Lovell, Wyoming, and many other concerned citizens, this area was set aside to help preserve the unique type of horse found here. A non-profit enterprise called the Pryor Mountain Wild Mustang Center was also set up to educate visitors on the history of the feral horses and to help the public appreciate the herd dynamics of the horses.

Adapted for the mountains

Like most mustangs, Pryor Mountain horses are small and compact, most standing between 14 and 14.2 hands (142 cm/56 in and 147.5 cm/58 in).

Unlike the horses that range through the south-west, however, these herds have adapted to their mountain environment and are heavier boned and stockier than other mustangs.

They have straight or sometimes convex profiles, small muzzles, wide-set, intelligent eyes, small ears, slightly cresty necks and full manes. Their shoulders have good angle and are sloping, as are their croups, with lush, low-set tails. They have clean, solid bone in legs and hard, well-conformed feet.

Like the Arabian, some of these mustangs have only five lumbar vertebrae (or the fifth and sixth vertebrae are fused) as opposed to the six typical of most breeds. They are highly intelligent, quick to learn and brave. Their surefootedness makes them excellent choices for endurance and trail riding. Some of them are born naturally gaited, which is not surprising, because of their close genetic links with the Paso Fino horses of Central America.

Significance of colour

Pryor Mountain horses occur in a variety of vivid coat colours. Famed equine geneticist Dr Phil Sponnenberg, of the veterinary college of the Virginia Polytechnic and State University, noted that their coat colours further confirm their place in the Spanish horse world. One signature coat is a dun or grulla (mouse-grey), with a dorsal stripe down the spine and zebra markings along the backs of knees and hocks. Apricot and claybank (yellowish) duns, blacks, bays, sorrels, red and blue roans and even palominos can be found in the herds. Pinto (skewbald and piebald) horses are rare and a sign of impurity.

BELOW *Living, as they do, in rocky, mountainous terrain further improves the surefootedness of the herd.*

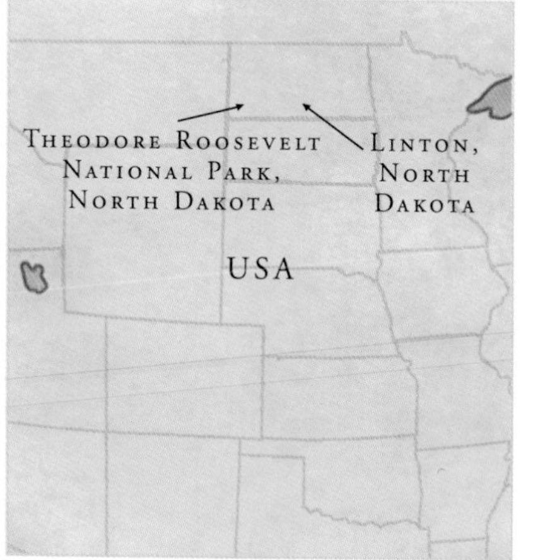

NOKOTA *horse*

TRAPPED IN A NATIONAL PARK

When the Theodore Roosevelt National Park was established in North Dakota in the 1950s, some of these wild horses were accidentally fenced in, setting in motion an unexpected chain of events. The National Park Service did not want them and tried to remove them, and it was only the intervention of two brothers during the 1980s that saved them from obscurity.

The badlands

Even the word 'badlands' conjures up a stark, remote, hostile environment and, in the rugged Little Missouri badlands of south-western North Dakota, conditions can indeed be harsh. There is little or no natural water, and summer temperatures hover around 35°C (95°F) while winter temperatures fall below -30°C (-20°F).

Today's Nokota horses are descended from generations of the last surviving mustangs that lived in this area. They have existed here for a hundred years, undisturbed until the mid-20th century.

Of Indian and Spanish extraction

The earliest horses to live in the Northern Plains were owned by Native American tribes. It is believed that the original horses of these plains were mostly of Spanish descent – originating in the south-western part of the

LEFT *The tangles in this wild horse's mane are called 'witches' knots'.*

ABOVE *The Nokota Horse Conservancy, the Kuntz family and others work to preserve and promote their breed.*

Americas and migrating north. The Spanish Barb and the Sorraia – both Colonial Spanish horses – were used by the native tribes, who trained them for war and for hunting buffalo on the northern grasslands. The tribes occasionally traded captured wild horses for these horses – or occasionally stole them during raids.

Sitting Bull's legacy

The early horses of the region had established their place in history, some of which is based in fact and some in folklore. After the Battle of Little Big Horn (also known as Custer's Last Stand), Sitting Bull, a Lakota medicine man, and some of his minor chiefs fled to Canada. Years later, in 1881, when Sitting Bull was forced to surrender to the US Army at Fort Buford, North Dakota, his party's horses were taken.

The army were unimpressed by these rough-looking 'Indian ponies', with their brightly coloured coats and small stature. They were certainly not in the class of the US Cavalry horses! Therefore they sold the horses to three post-traders: Leighton, Jordan and Hedderick. The Marquis de Mores, a flamboyant French aristocrat and pioneer rancher of western North Dakota, who was great admirer of the stamina of the Lakota tribe's horses, purchased 250 of them from the Fort Buford traders.

The Marquis founded the town of Medora, now the gateway to the Theodore Roosevelt National Park (TRNP). He intended to start a large breeding operation with these Indian horses and allowed them to run free on his land. When the Marquis died in 1896, the foreman of his ranch, John Goodall, rounded up as many horses as he could and sold them off. Not every horse left the area, however. Many had wandered further into the badlands, away from town, to start a free life.

Prisoners of the park

When the TRNP was first established, barbed-wire fencing was installed around the perimeter. Although the fencing of private land was making it increasingly difficult for wild horses to survive in western North Dakota, and although many horses were destroyed by ranchers, those inside the park's boundaries were physically safe. However, by being trapped in the park, they lost their protective 'safety net' – the Wild Free-Roaming Horse and Burro Act of 1971.

The National Park Service (NPS) accepts no responsibility for wild horses and, between 1950 and 1970, tried to remove all the horses from the park, selling most of them for slaughter, or even to be fed to captive lions and tigers. Public outcry eventually forced the NPS to stop the round-ups for slaughter and, instead, to keep a small 'historical demonstration herd' in the park, although they still sold off any excess horses.

During the 1980s, the NPS introduced outside breeds into the herds and culled any dominant park stallions. According to their reasoning, improving the horses' appearance would make them more valuable at auction.

The Kuntz brothers step in

With the horses being dispersed for sale or slaughter, as well as the cross breeding, the Nokota was in danger of elimination. Two brothers, Frank and Leo Kuntz, decided to purchase as many park horses as they could afford. As ranchers and horse breeders, they realised that the Nokota was a unique horse, worthy or preservation.

Unlike other horses from the area, the Kuntzes believed the Nokotas to be distinct in conformation and temperament, with historical significance. Author Castle McLaughlin was commissioned in 1989 to do a report on the horses. His findings were that the horses originated from Indian horses and settler's horses of the 20th century. He recommended that the park service safeguard these herds, not just because of their badlands heritage, but because their genetic hardiness should be preserved for generations to come.

However, the NPS elected to continue removing their feral horses, or 'Parkies'. For most of the following decade, the Kuntz brothers lobbied the NPS to change their policy and reinstate the original horses.

Meanwhile, the Kuntz herd was growing larger, threatening the brothers with bankruptcy. They bought the core of their herd in 1986 and selected horses at subsequent auctions up until 2001. By 1990, Frank and Leo had turned their lives over to caring for the horses, calling the horses 'Nokotas', a name that Leo created to indicate their North Dakota origins.

Because virtually all of the surviving Nokotas are now owned by the Nokota Horse Conservancy, the Kuntz family and other private individuals, the focus has shifted to preserving breeding stock and promoting their offspring as a new breed.

BELOW *The expressive faces of Nokotas gve them an air of intelligence.*

A colourful and intelligent horse

The Nokota is characterized by its colourful coat, which is often roan – usually blue or strawberry red, although some black roans are seen. It can also be bay or overo pinto (splashes of white on a solid background).

This horse has large, kind eyes, a broad forehead, and a long, thick mane and tail. It is highly intelligent and, unlike many feral horses, is curious rather than wary. It has a medium-sized head, with a straight or slightly concave profile, large eyes and hooked ears. Standing at 14.2–15 hands (147.5–152.5 cm/58– 62 in), it is large-boned, with a good angle to the shoulder, well-defined withers, a sloping croup, strong legs and tough hooves.

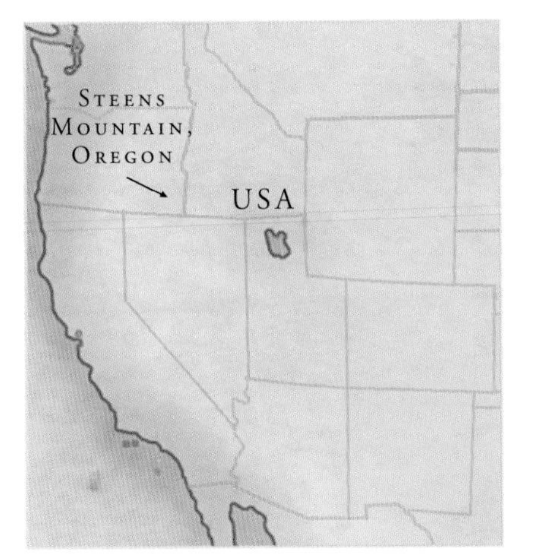

KIGER *mustang*

AN EXCITING DISCOVERY

Mustangs are usually associated with the American south-west, but one particular herd has thrived undisturbed for many years in the Pacific north-west, in the remote foot-hills of Oregon. These mustangs were only discovered in the 1970s, when they were given the name 'Kiger'. However, their ancestry can be traced back for centuries to the days of the Spanish explorers.

Spanish ancestry

In the 1500s, a large number of Spanish horses escaped from explorers or settlers, or were turned loose, and eventually formed wild bands. Throughout North America, these horses simply ran free. From time to time, other horses – horses that had broken loose from corrals, strayed or been set free – joined these bands of Spanish horses. All these different types of horses, from draught animals to fine-boned Thoroughbreds, ended up in the herds. The ones that survived the elements bred with the feral horses and their characteristics began to show up in the resulting foals.

As a result, horses with pure Spanish blood became more scarce. Occasionally, a foal known as a 'throwback' would be born, bearing the conformation and characteristics of the Spanish horses, but by the 1900s, most feral horses were a blend of hardy survivors, honed by their environment. In some areas of the US, however, small pockets of horses thrived in the safety of their isolated surroundings. These herds were full of what came to be known as Colonial Spanish horses.

LEFT *The Kiger herd is known for its horses with dun coats and black manes and tails.*

Above *Many private breeders are now helping the Kiger's numbers to gain strength.*

An Oregon home

While Oregon is best noted for its lush forests and breathtaking coastline, as well as its significant mountain ranges, much of the unpopulated area consists of prairie and deserts. It was in the austere, isolated foot-hills that a small band of mustangs flourished, well away from any traces of humankind.

In 1971, the Wild Free-Roaming Horses and Burros Act put the Bureau of Land Management (BLM) in charge of mustangs. In order to keep herd numbers in check, the BLM conducted regular gathers so that members of the public could 'adopt' wild mustangs.

In 1977, one of the BLM's wild horse specialists, E. Ron Harding, attended an Oregon gather. Harding noticed a sizeable band of wild horses that all had rich dun coats, thick black manes, lush tails and dark legs. These horses had been discovered in the Kiger Gorge, near the Steens Mountain. Harding was intrigued by these and, suspecting them to be of Spanish descent, followed their movements. The BLM chose to divide the herd and re-release the horses into south-eastern Oregon. One part of the herd went into the Kiger Herd Management Area (HMA), while the other went to the Riddle HMA.

In the 1990s, blood samples from the horses were sent to the University of Kentucky for testing. The results confirmed that these horses showed a lineage from Spanish ancestors that was no longer present in other mustangs. There was consistency not only in their bloodline, but in their characteristics, and because of their stunning coats, these wild horses soon became much sought after.

The Kiger mustang and the Steens Kiger

The Kiger mustang is still found in the HMA areas of Oregon and, every so often, some become available for adoption through the BLM. Because they are so desirable, however, with more adopters than horses available, competition for them is fierce.

Several private breeders are now using once-feral Kigers as a foundation for their own operations. This takes some pressure off the BLM to take feral horses off the range. Also, unlike their wild brethren, domestically bred Kigers can be handled like any other saddle horse, so buyers do not have to cope with taming and training a feral animal.

Because of the BLM's philosophy that only horses born outside of captivity can be called a mustang, one Kiger registry, the Steens Mountain Kiger Registry, omits the word 'mustang' from its title. Horses born in captivity are simply called Kiger horses, and all wild-bred and captive-bred Kigers are known in their registry as Steens Mountain Kigers.

BELOW *The claybank coat is a unique sandy dun coat highlighted by black points and a dorsal stripe.*

A striking appearance

The Kiger is known for its rich dun coat and full black mane and tail. However, the Kiger shows variations in this oak-coloured coat, including a red dun, a grulla and 'claybank'.

Like its Spanish-bred cousins, the Kiger mustang is a compact, well-muscled horse, with an upright carriage, a well-set neck and sloping shoulder. The Kiger's face is noble and expressive, with hook-tipped ears and a straight, or even slightly convex (not dished) profile. Its full tail is also set low on its haunches. Most have primitive markings, such as zebra stripes on the legs and a dark dorsal stripe. In some, the mane is a blend of light and dark hair.

Living conditions in Oregon helped the Kiger develop strong bone and dense hoof walls, which makes it sound and surefooted. Like other mustangs, they are not tall horses, and most range from 13.2 to 15.2 hands (137 to 157.5 cm/54 to 62 in).

South America

Criollo *horse*

National horse of Argentina

The gauchos, the legendary cowboys of the Argentine Pampas, owe their prowess in the saddle largely to their amazing horses. These horses – known as the Criollo in Argentina and Uruguay, and as the Crioulo in Brazil, Costeño and Morochuco in Peru, Corralero in Chile and Llanero in Venezuela – are very important in the equestrian cultures of South America.

Life on the Pampas

The word *criollo* (pronounced *cree-oh-yoh*) literally means 'creole' and originally referred to people and animals of pure Spanish ancestry that were born in the Americas. The Criollo is directly descended from the horses that the Spanish conquistadors brought to South America in the 16th century, one of whom, Don Pedro Mendoza, was the founder of Buenos Aires. It is said that many were of Barb descent, although they also have traces of Sorraia and Garrano horses in their blood.

Many of these cavalry horses escaped or were turned loose into the Pampas, a vast grassland area stretching north, south and west from the delta of the Rio de la Plata near Buenos Aires. Some perished as a result of the inhospitable conditions, while others, those that were not fast or enduring enough to keep up with the herd, fell victim to predators. The ones that did survive, however, adapted to life on the Pampas. Over the next 400 years, the *baguales* (or feral horses) that survived the harsh winters and scorching

Left *This Criollo has many distinctive characteristics, including a visible sclera around the eye and leopard spots.*

ABOVE *The endurance of the Criollo is legendary; today they are still used to compete in long-distance races.*

summers bred, and each spring's crop of foals was that much stronger. They became immune to the diseases that had decimated their predecessors. Their numbers grew into the thousands, and many of the native people and settlers reported seeing giant herds surging over the grasslands.

After seeing the settlers with their horses, the native people captured some of these horses and learned to ride, thus discovering new freedoms and opportunities. They began to use the horses for transport, hunting, ranching and even for games. When they were not using the horses, they allowed them to run free on the plains, rounding them up when they were needed.

European influences

With more settlers moving in, and more cattle operations setting up, the face of the wild Pampas changed. In 1806, and then in 1825, the influx of European invaders into the region had their impact on the small Criollo. The horse, ideally suited for life on the plains of South America, was not fully appreciated. Imported French Percherons and English Thoroughbreds were introduced into the feral horse herds, resulting in larger crossbreds.

Not everyone wanted to change the attributes of the little horse. The gauchos, for example, had defined themselves by this athletic horse, with its incredible stamina and aptitude for working cattle. They spent their lives in the saddle riding over the Pampas, and it was said that a gaucho without a horse was like a man without legs. The gauchos thus developed into skilful horsemen, but they were not easy on their horses. Their methods were tough, but the Criollo's temperament was suited to accept this kind of training.

The Criollo today

The pure Criollo was beginning to disappear as a result of poor breeding practices and, by the late 1800s, it was becoming uncommon to see herds of feral Criollos. In 1917, the Sociedad Rural de Argentina was formed to protect the Criollo. As a result of their search, the society discovered that a tribe of native South Americans had a small herd of 200 purebred horses, and these became the cornerstone of the restoration of the breed's ailing numbers. In Uruguay, the Genealogical Registers were opened in 1929 and in 1941 the Uruguayan Criollo Horse Breeder's Society was founded.

The breed was originally called the Argentinian, but was then changed to the Argentine Criollo. Today the horse is just known as the Criollo, since the horses of Argentina and Uruguay are of the same type and ancestry.

Beautiful and enduring

The Criollo has an intelligent look about it and is easily trained. Standing at an average of 14.1 hands (145 cm/57 in), stallions and geldings must be between 13.2 hands (137 cm/54 in) and 14.3 hands (150 cm/59 in). The maximum and minimum heights for mares are 2 cm (about 1 in) less.

These robust horses have a powerful conformation, reflecting their tough, vigorous nature. They have sloping, strong shoulders with cresty, upright necks. Their legs are short and strong, with ample bone, flat knees and good hocks and pasterns. The back is short, with a sloping croup and brawny hindquarters. Many coat colours are found in the breed, although dun-coloured horses are arguably toughest. Many horses bear primitive markings, such as leopard spots and dorsal stripes, and zebra stripes on the legs.

The signature of the Criollo is its amazing endurance; some people argue that it has even better stamina than the famous desert Arabian horse.

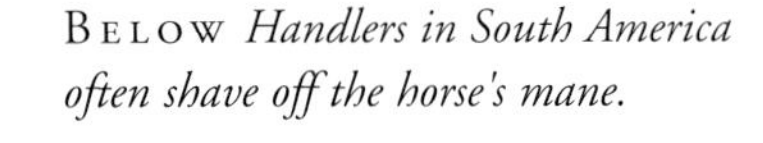

BELOW *Handlers in South America often shave off the horse's mane.*

Tests of endurance

The Criollo's endurance was put to the test by a Swiss professor and rider named A. F. Tschiffely in the 1920s. He rode from Buenos Aires in Argentina, through Central America, and into North America to Washington DC – a distance of more than 21,000 km (13,000 miles) – with two Criollo geldings. It took him more than 3 years to complete the journey, but the horses did well and even returned to Argentina as celebrities, to retire and live well into their 30s.

Each year the Criollo Breeders Association holds a 'raid', La Marcha, which in essence is an endurance ride to put the Criollo to the ultimate test of stamina. Each horse and rider must cover 750 km (465 miles) in 14 days. Horses must carry a minimum of 113 kg (250 lb) and can only eat and drink what they find along the route. A veterinarian checks the horses at the end of each day to determine whether they are fit enough to continue. This brutal ride determines which horses should pass their genes to another generation.

EUROPE

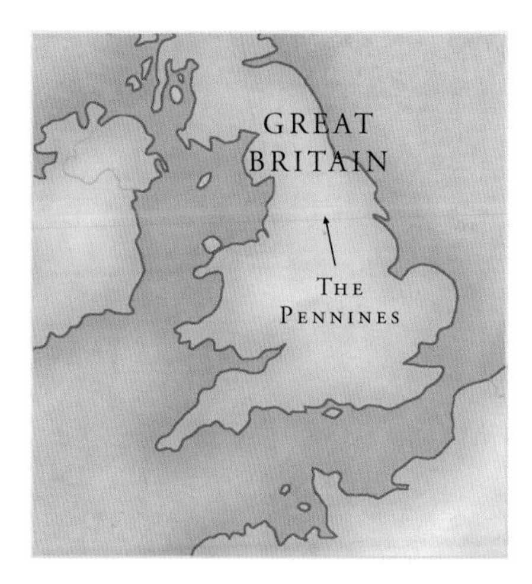

DALES *pony*

SURVIVOR IN NORTH-EASTERN ENGLAND

Like other native ponies of the British Isles, the Dales pony is an exceptional example of survival in an often hostile environment. Despite its uneasy existence – exposed to cold, rain, snow and wind, with poor food – it continues to thrive, and small herds still roam the upper dales of the rivers Tyne, Wear, Allen, Tees and Swale.

A mining background

The Dales pony is a native of the valleys, known as dales, of the eastern slopes of the Pennine hills in northern England, from High Peak in Derbyshire to the Cheviot Hills near the Scottish Border. Its origins lie with the ancient Pennine pony as well as the extinct Scottish Galloway, a hardy pony that bequeathed it speed and agility.

From the time of the Roman occupation until the mid-19th century, there was a flourishing lead-mining industry in this area of the Pennines. The native ponies were chosen to work in the mines because, although small, they had tremendous stamina and strength. They were used as pack ponies to transport heavy loads of lead from Northumberland and Durham to the smelting mills, and could cover up to 320 km (200 miles) in a week.

Dales ponies from the mines were also set to work on the small farms throughout the region, transporting both shepherds and hay to the flocks of sheep that were scattered over the fells. The rough country was difficult to traverse, but the surefootedness of the ponies meant that riders could be sure of reaching their destination safely.

LEFT *The Dales were bred to provide strength in a harsh environment.*

ABOVE *Living with no shelter, the Dales must endure each season's extremes.*

New roles

Breeders added other horses, such as the Norfolk Trotter, Yorkshire Roadster and, by some accounts, the Friesian, into the Dales herds in order to give them a little more substance. The infusion of trotting-horse blood had a unique side-effect: the Dales developed into a pony with a pretty knee action and the ability to race speedily at the trot. As a result, during the 18th century, the Dales pony became a formidable opponent in trotting races. Its endurance and agility also made it a favourite mount of the local hunts. The Dale's gait was further improved when a Welsh Cob Comet stallion was bred to Dales mares. Later in the same century, improvements to the roads of northern England created a demand for faster animals to pull mail coaches – and the quick little Dales pony fitted the bill.

In the 18th and 19th centuries, the Dales pony also found use as a military horse, and many were bred with the Clydesdale to create a draught pony. But in the 1900s, World War II took its toll on the Dales' population. Countless numbers were pressed into service as artillery horses, and many never returned from battle. Even worse, with so much cross-breeding, the purebred Dales pony was being bred out of existence. As a result, the numbers dwindled significantly. It was not until 1963, when the Dales Pony Society was formed out of the earlier Dales Pony Improvement Society, that breed numbers began to slowly increase.

A true survivor

Even the rampant cross-breeding and hard times has not diminished the qualities of the Dales pony. Today, the pony still has the traits that helped it to thrive in the uplands of the north-east.

Hardy, thrifty, sensible and strong, the modern Dales pony is not very different from the native ponies that roamed the Pennines centuries ago. Standing at about 14 hands (142 cm/56 in), these ponies are stout, muscular and beautiful. They are usually black or dark brown, although occasionally bay, grey or even roan ponies are found.

They have expressive, well-shaped heads with straight profiles, small muzzles and wide-set eyes. They are refined through the throatlatch and have short, arched upright necks, set on good sloping shoulders. Their legs are clean, with good substance and feathering below the knees. Strong loins and hindquarters give the Dales ponies excellent power, and their well-sprung ribcages allow ample room for the lungs to expand, which aids endurance. The hooves, which are large, round, and open at the heels, are usually of blue horn and very strong. A signature of the Dales pony is its full, lush mane and very long, thick tail.

BELOW *The Dales' thick manes, tails and leg 'feathering' offer protection from the elements.*

DARTMOOR *pony*

DEVON'S ANCIENT MOORLAND PONY

Dartmoor covers an area of 953 km² (368 sq. miles) in the south-west of England and its highest point, High Willhays, is 621 m (2,038 ft) above sea level. The soil is typically thin and acidic, interspersed with barren outcrops of weathered granite, known as tors. With little forage or protection from the Atlantic gales, the Dartmoor pony roams freely over the moor.

Compact and powerful

The Dartmoor pony is similar to the Exmoor (see pages 90–93). It stands at 11.1–12.2 hands (114.5–127 cm/45–50 in) and is compact and powerful.

Most ponies are brown, bay, black, grey, chestnut or even roan, but any 'coloured' ponies (piebald or skewbald) represent a partbred and are therefore ineligible for registration. Its head is small, with wide-set, intelligent eyes and alert ears, and its legs are short, with good, flat bone and hard, flinty hooves. They have good angular shoulders and well-developed hindquarters, which produce a nice movement at all gaits. The ponies have lush manes and tail.

A royal past

LEFT *Small but extremely hardy, the Dartmoor's history dates back nearly ten centuries.*

The Dartmoor pony, one of the nine native British breeds, has lived in the south-west of England for centuries. One of the earliest records of these ponies dates from 1012, when they were mentioned in the will of Awlfwold

ABOVE *In the 1930s, Dartmoor ponies numbered nearly 26,000; currently there are only 5,000 remaining.*

of Crediton, a Saxon bishop. Nearly a hundred years later, during the reign of Henry I, when Dartmoor was a royal forest, a stallion was taken from the forest and bred with the king's royal mares.

Not all of the pony's history with reigning monarchs was favourable. In 1535, King Henry VIII dealt a severe blow to the Dartmoor pony, and to the other native British ponies, when he passed a law to eliminate 'nags of small stature'. This was because of the need to breed large horses for war – infused with draught-horse blood – that could carry the weight of a soldier wearing the heavy armour of the times. Anyone found using a stallion under 14 hands (142 cm/56 in) was fined severely.

Six years later, in 1541, he passed another law prohibiting the use of any horse under 15 hands (152.5 cm/60 in), and the smaller ponies were gathered up and slaughtered. Fortunately, these laws were later annulled by Queen Elizabeth I. The ponies also received a reprieve during the reign of Edward VII, as the king valued the Dartmoor pony for his polo teams.

A working pony

Despite its small size, the Dartmoor's strength, coupled with its surefootedness, made this pony a good choice for many tasks. Because the area was rich in tin, this pony was used during the Middle Ages to carry heavy loads across the moors to neighbouring villages. However, during the mining operations of the 18th century, breeders wanted to make the Dartmoor a better pit pony and introduced Shetland pony blood into the Dartmoor pony population.

Between 1789 and 1832, there were many ponies around, but very few were purebreds because of all the cross-breeding. The mines in the area eventually closed and, while some Dartmoor ponies were kept for work on farms, most were turned loose, to find their way on the moors.

New records, new roles

In 1898, the Polo and Riding Pony Society in the UK started tracking the ponies in their studbook, and later, in 1924, the Dartmoor Pony Breed Society was founded, along with its own studbook. Numbers of the ponies were strong at this time, with an estimated 25,800 registered in the 1930s.

Dartmoor was noted for its high-security prison and, at the beginning of the 20th century, Dartmoor ponies were bred for prison work. Until the mid-20th century, they were used by the prison guards to escort prisoners who were participating in outside work programmes. These ponies were not always purebred, or even registered. By the time of World War I and World War II, there were fewer ponies on the books, because fewer were being bred. After the wars, diligent pony enthusiasts tried to make up for lost time and, by the 1950s, the numbers of Dartmoor ponies slowly began to increase.

Life in Dartmoor National Park

In 1951, Dartmoor was officially designated a national park. However, the quality of the ponies in the park had declined; since farmers allowed all kinds of horses and ponies to roam together, a pony in the park was not necessarily a Dartmoor pony. In 1988, The Dartmoor Pony Moorland Scheme was founded to help the purebred pony recover from its dangerously low numbers. The scheme places a herd of approved Dartmoor broodmares with a purebred Dartmoor stallion for the summer, and allows them to live in 'newtakes', a protected area of the park. This has resulted in the foaling of good purebred colts and fillies, and also benefits the park, because tourists come to see the ponies.

Organizers hope that the majority of the fillies born through this programme, who are upgraded after inspection, will return to the scheme and eventually replace the original mares. This will give breeders new horses in the gene pool, which is essential to the success of future breeding efforts. Despite this, and despite the fact that there are breeders all round the world; there are currently only about 5,000 Dartmoor ponies.

In Dartmoor National Park, some of the ponies are owned and protected by farmers and are usually identified by unique brands. Visitors to the park are prohibited from feeding the ponies, although this park law is often broken as many misguided people take pleasure in feeding biscuits and crisps to the ponies through their car windows.

BELOW *While various breeds can be seen in current Dartmoors, organisations are working to produce more purebreds.*

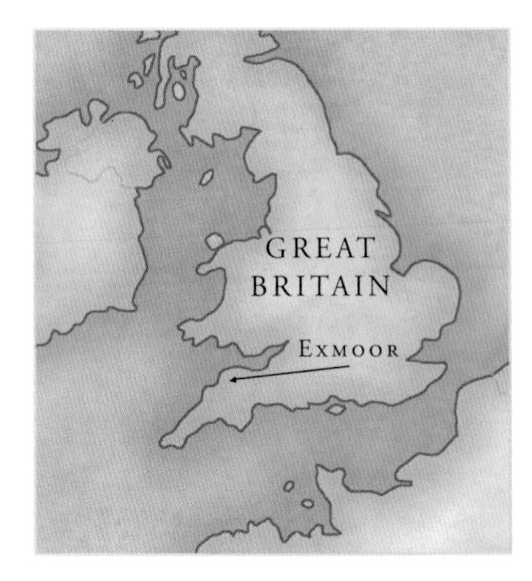

EXMOOR *pony*

BRITAIN'S LINK WITH THE PAST

The Exmoor pony is the oldest and purest of British native pony breeds. A direct descendant of the Celtic pony that migrated from North America to Europe, it has been so sculpted by the demands of its new environment that it is often described as the 'child of the moor'.

A moorland home

Exmoor lies on the northern coast of south-western England where Devon and Somerset border the Bristol Channel. About a quarter of this area consists of uncultivated heath and moorland, either covered in fragrant heather or swathed in various species of grasses and sedges. Some of the highest and loneliest moorland on Exmoor is found in The Chains, where Dunkery Beacon, at 519 m (1,704 ft), is the highest peak. This is the home of the Exmoor pony, which can be seen roaming freely on the moors.

Child of the moor

This intelligent, alert and tractable pony is consistent in both coat colour and conformation. They are usually dark brown in colour, with black manes, black tails and black legs, although there are also duns and bays. The bays, however, do not display the white facial markings, typical of such colouring, although they do tend to sport a lighter fawn-coloured muzzle and eyes – a colouring known as 'mealy'.

LEFT *Due to isolation and climate, with time and natural selection the Exmoor became a tough, resilient equine.*

All Exmoors have sizeable heads, with wide-set, expressive eyes, straight profiles, small ears and deep jaws with good throatlatches. The body is compact, with an ample barrel, powerful haunches, a short back and a round croup. The legs are short, with clean joints and sturdy bone, and good, hard hooves. The shoulders are well laid back, which produces little knee action, giving it a smooth stride rather than a short, choppy gait.

Stallions and geldings generally stand at 11.3–12.3 hands (119.5–129.5 cm/ 47–51 in), while mares stand at 11.2–12.2 hands (117–127 cm/46–50 in) for mares. The average weight is 317–363 kg (700–800 lb).

Prepared for winter

Over the centuries, the Exmoor pony has developed two unusual characteristics that are found in only one or two feral breeds. The first is a 'hooded eye' – a heavy upper brow that protects the eye from strong wind and rain, and often gives the Exmoor a toad-like appearance, and the second is an 'ice tail' – a fan of top tail hairs that allow rain to sheet off the body and keep the belly dry, also found in the Icelandic pony.

The Exmoor also grows a dense haircoat during the winter, with an underlayer of downy hair that insulates the body. The coat is so perfectly engineered for bad weather that the top layer has special oils that also act as

BELOW *Even tiny foals bear the unique toad, or hooded, eye to protect them from lashing winds and rain.*

ABOVE *The Exmoor is perfectly adapted to a life that is often difficult on the moors.*

waterproofing, so that the ponies do not get soaked to the skin. Both the ice tail and the coat are shed every spring, leaving the Exmoor sleek and gleaming.

Isolated past

Evidence shows that the Exmoor pony is descended directly from the ancient Celtic pony, a small equine that migrated from North America into Europe, across the prehistoric land bridge, about 130,000 years ago. As early as 1,000 BC, Celtic ponies bred with European native horses throughout the region.

Records from the 1500s and onwards show that the number of ponies on Exmoor fluctuated, with the population sometimes rising to as many as a thousand or more. At this time, Exmoor, a property of the Crown, was a royal forest and hunting ground. It was controlled by wardens, who ran native stallions in the forest and occasionally put in other breeds within the herds.

By the 1700s, because of its intelligence and easy-going nature, the Exmoor pony had acquired several roles, including hunting and farm use. In 1818, the Crown sold the royal forest to John Knight, and there was a dispersal sale for the ponies. The last warden of Exmoor, Sir Thomas Acland, took 30 of the ponies and established the Acland Herd (now known as the Anchor Herd), whose descendants still live on Winsford Hill.

Local farmers who had worked with Acland also bought ponies at the dispersal sale and founded several new herds, which helped to keep the pony's bloodlines pure. John Knight attempted to breed more refinement and size into the Exmoor pony and released an Arabian stallion on to the moors. The resulting foals, however, lacked the traits necessary to survive the harsh life on the moors and the offspring eventually died out in the early 1900s.

20th-century troubles

The Exmoor Pony Society was formed in 1921, with the aims of preserving and protecting the purebred Exmoor pony. The breed's numbers increased until World War II, when its fortunes changed dramatically: troops in training on the moors often used the ponies for target practice, and many ponies were killed for food. A severe winter followed and, by the spring of 1948, there were only about 50 Exmoor ponies left.

However, concerned breed enthusiasts, particularly Mary Etherington, helped to ensure that the existing ponies were given a fighting chance of survival and the breed's fortunes shifted once again.

The numbers of Exmoor ponies remained low until the early 1980s, when a publicity campaign drew outside attention to the rarity of the breed. Two types of Exmoor still exist today: the Acland type (see above), and the Withypool type (a slightly larger, darker pony with a straighter profile).

NEW FOREST *pony*

A PEOPLE'S PONY

While this pony lives a free-roaming existence in the New Forest area of southern England, it is not a typical feral horse. Although untamed, it lives in close proximity to the local people, with whom it has a special and sometimes uneasy relationship, governed by an historic system of legislation.

A royal forest

The New Forest, which lies in the counties of Hampshire and Wiltshire, between Southampton and Bournemouth, is one of the largest unenclosed stretches of countryside in southern England (about 243 km², or 94 sq. miles, in area). It was created in 1079 as a deer-hunting area by King William I, best known as William the Conqueror. At that time, the word 'forest' referred to an area that was subject to Forest Law rather than a wooded area, and much of it still consists of open heath, grassland and bog.

Over the centuries, the forest has undergone many changes according to the whims of the ruling monarch. However, because the soil in the New Forest is not fertile enough for agriculture, the ponies have been left largely undisturbed. Much of the original forest, which was declared a National Park in March 2005, is still owned by the Crown.

In the days of William I, the Crown's main priority was the needs of the deer, but it also made some allowances for the needs of the inhabitants. The local villagers were given the rights to graze their herds of horses, cattle and pigs, to dig clay and to gather timber for fuel under the Rights of Common,

LEFT *New Foresters are among the most approachable of all the native British pony breeds.*

ABOVE *Attempts to improve the breed actually resulted in ponies that didn't thrive so well in the Forest.*

and therefore became known as commoners. These ancient Forest rights are still in force today.

The New Forest pony was recorded as roaming the area six decades before the founding of the forest by King William I. In a true sense, they have played as large a part in shaping their forest as the forest has played in shaping them. Grazing freely in the forest, the ponies (along with the cattle and pigs) eat what they find palatable and leave what they cannot eat. As a result, the forest vegetation is defined by what the animals leave behind, and the ponies become hardy because they survive on what little nutrition is found in the native plants.

Shaped by the forest

The upper height limit of the New Forest pony is 14.2 hands (147.5 cm/ 58 in) but there is no lower limit, although ponies are seldom under 12 hands (122 cm/48 in). They should have conformation for riding rather than driving. Foresters have good angles to the shoulder, powerful haunches, broad through the body, ample bone and hard hooves. All coat colours are permitted except piebald, skewbald (pinto) and blue-eyed cream.

Improving the breed

Over the centuries, other horses were introduced into the herds of New Forest ponies in order to improve the breed. Arabian, Hackney and Thoroughbred blood was occasionally added to get taller horses and refine the breed. However, while the new blood did indeed add refinement, many of these newly introduced horses died out because they were not genetically equipped to cope with the sparse forage in winter. In the 19th century, a better effort was made to refine the ponies. One of Queen Victoria's Arabian stallions, 'Zorah', was turned loose on the heathland between 1852 to 1860 in order to improve the breed.

Pony enthusiasts formed a society in 1891 to record the pedigrees of the New Forest ponies. The society started registering ponies in 1906 and, in 1910, the Burley and District New Forest Pony and Cattle Breeding Society published their first studbook. During that time, it was thought that other native pony stallions could help to improve the breed, so Highland and Fell ponies were introduced, along with Dartmoor, Exmoor and Welsh ponies. The practice was eventually stopped and no outside breeds have been allowed in the studbook since 1930.

BELOW *The most common colours are bay, brown and grey followed by chestnuts, roans and blacks.*

ABOVE *In order to be noted as Forest Bred, ponies must be sired and foaled on the open New Forest.*

Life in the New Forest

The officials in overall charge of the New Forest are called verdurers, but the day-to-day administration is carried out by the agisters, who are responsible for the ponies' welfare. The small group of agisters are experts both in the New Forest and the animals that live within. Each oversees one of five allocated areas and manages the ponies that live in their area.

The ponies form groups that occupy discrete areas of the Forest, commonly known as 'haunts', but this does not mean that the ponies do not head into the villages. One of the biggest challenges that the New Forest pony faces is to be roaming free but still in such close proximity to people. Unlike their shy, suspicious feral cousins, these ponies are often quite brazen. They are not particularly bothered by traffic and, as a result, many wander along both the roadsides and the roads. Consequently, many ponies are hit and killed by vehicles, while others are so badly injured that they must be destroyed. The number of livestock killed each year is increasing as the human population of the area, both residents and tourists, increases.

The agisters work hard to make the public aware that, despite their appearance, the ponies are semi-wild. Accidents often occur due to people trying to feed the ponies, and ponies frequently become ill when given unsuitable food. Ponies sometimes get too bold when it comes to 'treats', and a pony that injures a person is usually removed from the Forest permanently.

Natural and unnatural hazards

Litter is a major hazard for the ponies, whether it is left by tourists or comprises the contents of the villagers' bins. The ponies will tear into anything in search of a treat and may injure themselves on sharp cans or become ill from eating the wrong things. Most residents have learned to deal with this by locking their gates or their rubbish bins.

Ponies have also become ill, or even died, as a result of well-meaning people offering them lawn mowings or hedge clippings. Lawn mowings often ferment when eaten, releasing enough gas to rupture the animal's stomach and intestines, resulting in an agonizing death. Clippings from yew, laburnum, rhododendron, some conifers and azaleas, as well as many other garden plants, are poisonous to animals so residents are told to dispose of garden waste carefully rather than dumping it in the forest.

The ponies have also come to serious harm through natural curiosity or the search for food. Residents in the New Forest are legally obliged to fence their properties in order to keep the ponies out. This means that property-owners cannot claim compensation from the owner of a pony that gets in through a gap in their fence or an open gate and tramples their beautiful lawn or eats their shrubs. On the other hand, the pony's owner can claim compensation if a pony is injured or poisoned in a property-owner's garden. There have been incidents of ponies falling into swimming pools (especially ones covered with plastic sheeting) where, apart from the poor animal drowning, the pony's owner has successfully sued.

Dogs are also a problem. Every year they injure New Forest ponies, particularly young foals. Some are even killed or die later from infected bites.

The New Forest pony today

New Forest ponies continue to graze throughout the forest, and registered stallions are released into the forest between April and July to continue the breed. Ponies born in the New Forest are referred to as 'forest-bred'. Forest-bred ponies are sold at the Beaulieu Road Sales, which are held throughout the year. New Forest ponies are also bred at private studs in the New Forest and countrywide.

BELOW *All the New Forest ponies have owners and are watched over by forest agisters.*

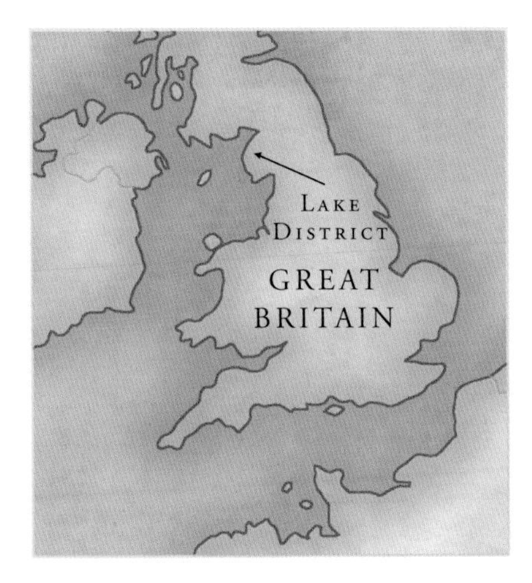

FELL *pony*

HARDY PONY OF NORTHERN BRITAIN

One of the nine native British pony breeds, the hardy Fell pony is another prime example of a pony being a product of its environment. Exposed to howling winds, biting rain, rocky, rough terrain, and with little forage for nourishment, the Fell reflects its inhospitable home territory by being equally tough and enduring.

Ancient origins

The Fell pony first appeared on British soil as an ancient forest-type pony that crossed the land bridge from North America into Europe, and then into Britain, during the Ice Age in about 15,000 BC. These ponies dispersed throughout Britain, with groups settling into a variety of different habitats that gradually helped to shape their current attributes. One group, the Fell ponies, named after the hills of the Lake District in Cumbria, northern England, had to survive often harsh conditions. The weather, with its short rainy summers and long cold winters, created ponies that could thrive under these dismal conditions.

The Fell pony is often mistakenly referred to as a 'miniature Friesian' but, while the pony may share some similar outward characteristics with its larger Dutch compatriot, the Friesian does not appear to be a major player in the Fell pony's history.

LEFT *With their dark coats, long manes and tails and feathering, many consider Fells to be 'small Friesians.'*

According to some reports, mercenaries in the Roman army crossed Friesian stallions with native ponies during the building of Hadrian's Wall in AD 120. (This wall, which stretches from coast to coast, approximately along the border of England with Scotland, was intended to prevent warring Pictish tribes entering Roman-occupied Britain.) However, studies comparing the Fell pony with equine fossils from Hadrian's Wall and other places show no evidence of this. Also, the Friesian as we know it today did not exist during Roman times, and the horses brought by the Romans were probably relatives of the Fell pony that shared the same prehistoric ancestors.

The now-extinct Scottish Galloway, a pony ridden by Scottish raiders, is also thought to have been very similar to the Fell pony and may even have been absorbed into native Fell pony stock. However, trying to separate the early history of the two can be confusing because 'galloway' was an old name given to any draught-type of pony.

Built for work

The Fell pony retains many of its unique prehistoric forest-pony characteristics. The thick forelock and mane and feathers on the legs help to shed water away from the skin, and the large hooves help to prevent the pony from sinking into the soft ground. The sloping shoulders and rounded hindquarters, which made the pony nimble in the boggy forest floor, today make the pony move with a comfortable, easy gait.

With strong haunches and muscular thighs, the Fell is a heavy-boned sturdy pony, able to carry heavy loads. Although its temperament is lively, it is known for its level-headedness. Fell ponies are also noted for their longevity.

It stands at 12.2–13.3 hands (127–139.5 cm/50–55 in) and the most common colour is black, although brown, bay and pale grey are also seen. White markings are acceptable, although a small star or socks are preferred to blazes or stockings.

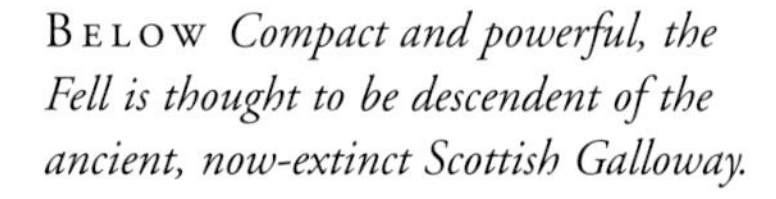

BELOW *Compact and powerful, the Fell is thought to be descendent of the ancient, now-extinct Scottish Galloway.*

Traditional uses

The Cumbrian farmers needed a utility animal to work the hilly landscape. Large draught horses, although perfect for working extensive, flat swathes of land, were not much use on the steep slopes of their small hill farms. However, working on these slopes was second nature to the Fell ponies, and their willingness made them perfect for the farmers' uses: pulling hay rakes, mowing machines and hauling carts. Many farmers used the ponies for shepherding – riding them to their flocks and back again.

During the Industrial Revolution, Fell ponies were used to carry coal out of the fells. Their calm, unflappable nature, in addition to both their strength and agility, made them very easy to handle, and it was not unusual to see as many as 20 ponies with only one person in charge of the entire group.

ABOVE *Fells are normally black, although bay, brown and pale grey are seen as well.*

In 1893 a studbook was established in the UK to record and register ponies. The Fell Pony Society of the UK was founded in 1916 by hill-farmers, Fell-pony admirers and the Earl of Lonsdale.

After World War II, increased mechanization meant fewer jobs for the ponies. Recreational riding remained a pastime only of the well-to-do, so the ponies were either sold to slaughterhouses or were no longer bred. Their numbers fell dramatically and the Fell pony seemed set for extinction until the early 1980s, when riding became more generally popular throughout the UK. To increase their numbers, the Fell Pony Society received funding from Queen Elizabeth II and a grant from the Horse Race Betting Levy Board to subsidize breeders and help shoulder their costs.

A changing role

Although some Fell ponies are still used as general work ponies, many others are used for driving and riding. One particular sport where the ponies truly shine is in combined carriage-driving. Ponies are particularly sought after by amateurs and professionals alike as they are cheap to keep, easy to keep fit and, because of their small size, extremely nimble and manoeuvrable in cross-country work. The Duke of Edinburgh, husband of Queen Elizabeth II, drives a team of four Fell ponies in international competition.

Queen Elizabeth herself, a great admirer of this native English pony, both owns and breeds Fells. As patron of the Fell Pony Society, she donates generously to it each year and consults with its council members, even inviting them to her various homes for discussions and tours of the premises.

On her Scottish estate of Balmoral, her ponies are used after stag hunts to transport the carcasses off the moors. For the Balmoral gamekeepers, who need to cull more than 700 deer every year in order to maintain a healthy population of animals, it is a challenge, if not impossible, to transport all the carcasses off the moors, even with all-terrain vehicles. The Queen's Fell ponies provide the perfect solution.

The Fell pony today

In the UK, there are fewer than 500 breeding mares and 100 stallions, and the Fell pony is on the endangered list of the Rare Breeds Survival Trust. There are also fewer than 100 breeding animals in the US, and fewer than 5,000 Fell ponies world-wide. The ponies are most popular in the UK, the Netherlands, France, Germany and North America.

Fifteen herds still run wild in the Cumbrian hills. The ponies have owners, but the Department for Environment, Food and Rural Affairs (Defra) has classed the ponies as semi-feral. Each spring the ponies are brought down to the lowlands to be supervised as they foal. Fell-pony enthusiasts wish to keep the herds on their native habitat for two reasons: ponies raised on the fells tend to keep their native hardiness intact, and for the sake of tradition.

HIGHLAND *pony*

PONY OF THE SCOTTISH HIGHLANDS

Protected by its dense coat, this sturdy pony has thrived for centuries in the windswept valleys, around the lochs and along the coast of the Scottish highlands. One of Britain's nine native pony breeds, two of which are found in Scotland, the Highland pony has a long history, perhaps dating from before the last Ice Age.

Galloway greatness

Evidence shows that an ancient pony lived in the Highlands perhaps as long as 10,000 years ago. Over the centuries, this prehistoric pony was changed by breeding with other ponies belonging to whichever army was currently invading the area. The Galloway pony featured quite prominently in the ancestry of the Highland pony.

In the 18th and 19th centuries, although the basic bloodline of the ponies remained the same, their regional isolation on the islands, or perhaps in the glens, resulted in different strains of ponies, including the Islay, Rhum, Mull and Barra strains. The Eriskay pony (see pages 108–111), far west in the Hebrides, was considered a lighter type of Highland pony.

Two distinct types began to appear: one was the small, sturdy, lightly built island pony, while the other was the stout, powerfully built pony from the mainland, referred to as a Garron in Gaelic. In the 18th century, Iberian horses as well as the French draught horse, the Percheron, found their way to the Scottish highlands. Later, in the 19th century, Dales ponies and also a carriage type of Hackney and Fell were added to the Highland gene pool.

LEFT *The Highland is the largest of the nine British native pony breeds.*

ABOVE *Power and surefootedness made the Highland a favourite for hunters in the Scottish hills, who used them to bring back stags, which can weigh up to 100 kg (about 225 lb).*

In the 18th century, many stud farms sprang up over the countryside, the most notable being the Duke of Atholl's stud. At the end of the 19th century the Faille stud on the Scottish island of Skye was founded, to breed ponies for farm work. Later, in 1913, the stud was moved to Inverness and changed its name to Knocknagael. Over the decades this stud became famous for the many quality ponies that were bred there but, because the stud was government owned, it was closed due to budget cuts in December 1977. However, breed society members snapped up the ponies at sale, so the breed suffered no ill effects.

Strong and sturdy

The Highland pony is on the large side, because its two different types have merged over the years to produce one distinct type. It stands at 13–14.2 hands (137–147.5 cm/54–58 in) and has a pretty head, with alert eyes, small ears, a broad muzzle and deep jowls. This is set on a slightly arched, well-developed medium-length neck. The back is of medium length, while the withers are fairly well defined and the shoulder is deep, long and sloping.

The conformation of the body shows its power, from the well-muscled hindquarters to the deep chest and broad ribcage. The legs are blessed with solid bone and muscle, and have dark, well-formed, sturdy hooves. Both mane and tail are long, thick and lush, and the fetlocks bear silky feathering.

Some of the traits of the Highland pony reveal its primitive origins. Their coats come in a variety of colours, but most, such as dun, grey, brown, black, chestnut and cream, are found in other horses that have ancient origins. Some exhibit a dorsal stripe and zebra striping, and some even have shoulder stripes. Any extra white is usually an indication of past cross-breeding, and Highland stallions cannot be registered if they show more than a small white star. Likewise, spotted ponies not eligible for the registry.

A hard worker

The ponies of the Highlands were originally bred to help farmers, whether by carrying game from the mountains, ploughing the fields or hauling wood from the forest. The ponies could live outside in all weather, all year round. They had heavy winter coats, consisting of a layer of strong, badger-like hair over a soft dense undercoat, which they shed in late spring, revealing short, glossy summer coats. Most of all, farmers liked them because they were easily trained, sensible and, mostly, unflappable.

The Scottish Highlands have a long history of strife, so it not surprising that the Highland pony was used both by warring clans and, later, by the army, even during World War II. Highland ponies are practically synonymous with the sports of stalking and shooting.

Royal connections

The Highland pony has had a long and illustrious relationship with the royal family, from Queen Victoria to the present Queen, Elizabeth II. Her Majesty is patron of the breed society and has a personal interest in both showing and breeding Highlands. She currently has one of the largest working studs of Highland ponies. During the season, more than 20 of her ponies can be seen regularly on the hillsides around Balmoral Castle, in Aberdeenshire, carrying grouse, deer, people and lunch, as well as hacking out or driving. With two stallions ('Balmoral Dee' and 'Balmoral Moss') and a broad-based line of mares, the Balmoral stud consistently produces quality foals, ensuring the future of the breed.

BELOW *Some of the most exquisite Highlands in the world make their home at the Balmoral Castle stud.*

The Highland pony today

There are an estimated 5,000 to 6,000 Highland ponies worldwide, mainly in Scotland, but many also in England, with a few elsewhere in the British Isles.

Unlike many of Britain's native ponies, the Highland pony is not required to undergo an inspection in order to receive registration. There are no stringent breeding rules, whereby a breeder must use only an approved or selected stallion, so the Highland pony is able to draw from a larger gene pool. While this means that it shows plenty of variation in size, coat colour and even conformation, it is still the result of centuries of breeding for practical purposes, rather than for any loftier reason.

ERISKAY *pony*

LIFE IN THE SCOTTISH ISLANDS

The Eriskay pony is the last survior of the original native ponies of the Western Isles of Scotland. Its lineage goes back to the days of the ancient Norse and Celtic peoples. Intricate likenesses of the pony can be seen among the symbols on the tall, ornately carved Pictish stones that were erected in the area in about the 8th century.

An island home

Eriskay, which derives its name from the Old Norse word *Eirisgeidh*, meaning 'Eric's Isle', lies off the north-western coast of Scotland and is one of the chain of islands known as the Western Isles (or Outer Hebrides). Most of these islands are inhabited only by wildlife, although some of the more accessible islands also have a human population.

The island of Eriskay, which is only about 5 km (3 miles) long and 3 km (2 miles) across at its widest point, is a combination of rough, rocky terrain and sandy beaches. For centuries, it has been home to a small community of crofters, mainly fishermen, who also cultivated the meagre soil.

Eriskay has a rich and colourful history. While it is well-known for the traditional Hebridean song, the 'Eriskay Love Lilt', and the seamless Eriskay jersey, it is also the site of two particular important historical events: it was here that Bonnie Prince Charlie landed with his 'seven men of Moidart' to launch the 1745 Jacobite Rising; and it was here that the SS *Politician*, with its cargo of whisky, ran aground in 1941, providing the inspiration for the book and subsequent film *Whisky Galore*.

LEFT *The northern-most native pony of Great Britain, the Eriskay pony's home is remote and isolated.*

ABOVE *Eriskay ponies are often born black, dark brown or bay and then lighten to grey as they age, although some stay dark throughout their lives.*

A crofter's pony

The ponies on Eriskay were captured and set to work on the 'crofts' – small areas of enclosed farmland with a dwelling-place, managed by tenant farmers. These ponies were used by the crofters to work the land, haul peat and generally as a family pony.

Life was hard for a crofter's pony: as well as putting up with the dismal weather conditions, living in boggy mud and being pelted by constant rain, it also had to endure long days of hard work. In addition, there was little feed for the ponies, so the ability to exist and work daily on the sparse forage was key to their survival. Tractability ensured a pony's future; any ponies that were hard to train, or ill-tempered, were culled from the herd.

Powerful and hardy

These conditions helped to shape the modern Eriskay pony. Although small and quite refined, this pony, which stands at 12.0–13.2 hands (122–137 cm/ 48–54 in), is quite powerful and hardy for its stature.

Its coat grows thick and dense in the winter months, serving as insulation from the cold and wet. Like the ice tail of the Icelandic pony, the tail fans out over the dock area, providing warmth and protection to the hindquarters, and the slight silky feathering on the cannon bones protects the legs from brambles and thorny vegetation.

Eriskay ponies are commonly born black, dark brown or bay, but they often lighten to grey as they age, although some ponies keep their dark coats throughout their life.

Changing times

Until 2001, when a causeway between Eriskay and South Uist was built, the island was isolated from the mainland. Consequently, the Eriskay pony as a breed was not subjected to any human interference. However, their purity became a double-edged sword. With the decline in agriculture in the 20th century, breeding of the ponies ceased and, by the late 1960s, there were only about 25 Eriskay ponies on the island.

Some islanders from a local village – including farmers, veterinarians, a priest and a scientist – joined together to produce a plan to save the remnants of the once-flourishing herd. They diligently put together a breeding programme, which now operates throughout the UK, and as a result about 420 ponies are now thriving.

The Eriskay Pony Society, which was established in 1995 to preserve and protect the future of the breed, promotes shows and various competitions, as well as offering breeding advice. An offshoot of this society, the Eriskay Pony (Mother Society), or *Comann Each nan Eilean*, focuses purely on breeding ponies in the Western Isles.

Today, visitors can see ponies roaming on Eriskay and also on Holy Isle, in the Firth of Clyde, the northern part of which is designated as a nature reserve, and which has free-roaming Eriskay ponies, Saanen goats, Soay sheep and various rare species of native flora.

BELOW *Despite steps to preserve them, Eriskays are still critically endangered and constantly fighting extinction.*

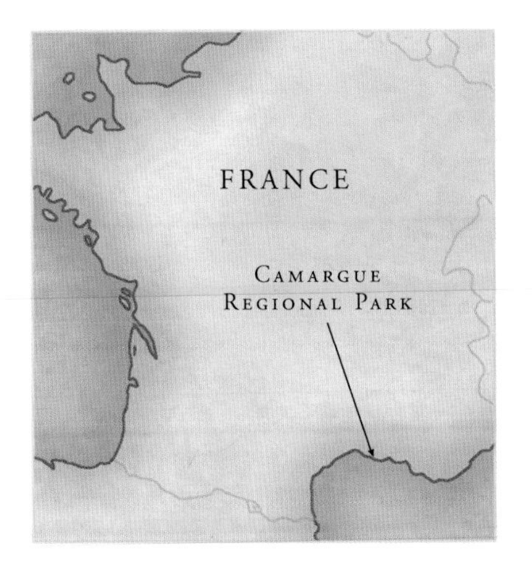

CAMARGUE *horse*

WILD HORSE OF THE WATER

A herd of these pale horses, foraging among the long grasses of the Rhône delta, is an unforgettable sight. They seem unaffected by the heat, or the biting insects, which they swish away with their tails. Instead, they seem to thrive in this harsh environment and have an otherworldly quality, as if they could disappear into the marshland at any moment.

A long history

The feral Camargue horse, the 'horse of the sea', is an ancient breed that has lived on the marshy plains of the Rhône delta in southern France since prehistoric times. Some experts believe that the Camargue originated from the long-extinct Soutré horse, whose skeletons (dating from 17,000 years ago) are scattered throughout south-eastern France. Others claim that the Camargue horse is of Arab or Saracen descent, originating from Arabian horses that were cast into the wild during the barbarian invasion of southern France in the 8th century.

The Celts and Romans who invaded the Iberian Peninsula found much to appreciate in the Camargue horse and, as a result, the horse's bloodlines became intertwined with some of the Spanish breeds, particularly those in the northern part of the peninsula. The influence of the Camargue on other breeds soon became apparent, and horses such as the Spanish Jaca were probably a cross between the Celtic pony and the Camargue.

LEFT *The Camargue has the convex profile of more ancient breeds, yet some still show hints of Arabian and Thoroughbred.*

Shaped by the sea

The vast brackish lagoons of the Rhône delta, known as *étangs*, are separated from the Mediterranean sea by large sandbars. This area of briny ponds and waterways – nearly a third of which is marsh – is a perfect breeding ground for voracious mosquitoes and other biting pests. Over the centuries, the Camargue horses have adapted to these difficult conditions, thriving in spite of the sparse feed, the often unbearably humid summers and the freezing winters. It was this environment that helped them to develop into such athletic, hardy creatures of the wetlands. Although the breed has largely developed through natural selection, soldiers passing through the area have bred their own mounts to the Camargue, resulting in an overall improvement of the horses.

The Camargue horses still run wild in the marshes and are overseen by the Biological Station of la Tour du Valat. Horses are rounded up each year and some stallions are gelded. The Carmargue Regional Park acts as a reserve for the horses. In 1976, the French government set standards for the breed and started to register the main breeders of the Camargue horse, setting up a studbook in 1978. In order to be registered, foals must be born outdoors, as opposed to in a stable, and must be seen to suckle from a registered mare as proof of parentage. Foals born within the boundaries of the Camargue are registered as *sous berceau* (meaning 'in the birthplace'), while those born outside the region are registered as *hors berceau* (meaning 'outside the birthplace').

BELOW *Mutual grooming is a behaviour that almost all horses derive true pleasure from.*

The Camargue horse is small but hardy, and bears the large, convex profile of more ancient breeds. However, the presence of the blood of Thoroughbred and Arabian horses, and the Barb horses of Africa, is also apparent. The *gardians*, or French cowboys, who oversee the horses, live an austere life based on years of tradition. They round them up for annual inspections and brand and geld any stallions that are deemed unsuitable for breeding. Fillies are usually caught and branded as yearlings and colts deemed unsuitable for breeding are gelded when 3 years old. Breeding is semi-wild but under the supervision of the Biological Station of la Tour du Valat.

A horse of character

The Camargue has developed into a distinct type of horse: stocky, with stout legs, hooves and haunches. Its primitive features include a heavy mane and tail, and a large square head with large

Above *The marshy ground presents no problems for these well-adapted horses.*

eyes flush to the skull. It also has a short neck, a deep chest, pronounced withers, a short, straight back and a compact body overall. Natural selection has made these hardy horses slightly smaller than their domestically bred counterparts, and they stand at 13–14 hands (132–142 cm/52–56 in). Foals are born black or dark brown and fade to light grey or nearly white as they age.

These horses can travel for great distances, their broad hooves and sturdy legs enabling them to move easily over the marshy environment. They are also are able to survive on poor forage and in extreme conditions. Their teeth are adapted for eating tough marsh plants: in spring, the horses nip off reeds and a local species of samphire, while, in winter, when forage is sparse, they survive on goosefoot and dried grasses, which other grazers find inedible. They run in typical bands of one stallion, a lead mare and the rest of his mares and his offspring.

Because of their calm temperament, agility, intelligence and stamina, these horses are used for gymkhana games, dressage and also endurance racing, which is gaining favour in their native France. Traditionally, Carmargue horses are ridden by the local *gardians*, who also manage the black feral bulls of the region that are used for bull-fighting.

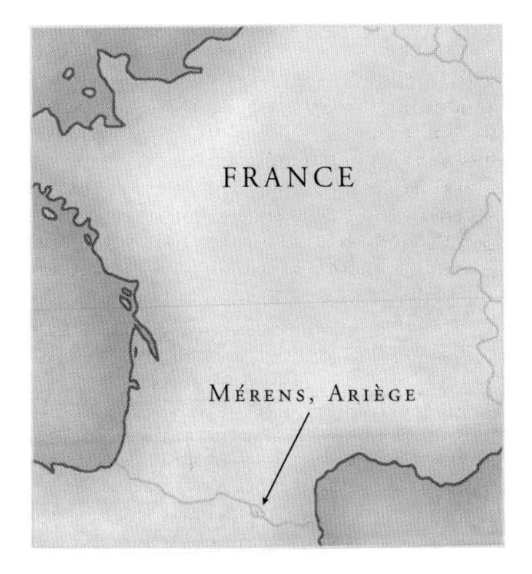

MÉRENS *horse*

THE BLACK PRINCE (*Prince Noir*) OF ARIÈGE

These dark, compact little horses make their home on the outskirts of Mérens, high in the Ariège Pyrenees, on the sheer, rock-strewn mountainside. Impervious to the bitter cold and the thin air, they are a perfect match for this rough terrain. They are surprisingly alike, all sharing the same shiny black coat and lush mane and tail.

Horse or pony?

One of the extraordinary traits of the Mérens is the similarity of individual horses. At 13.1–14.1 hands (134.5–145 cm/53–57 in), Mérens are jet black and look much like the British Fell pony or the Dutch Friesian horse. The Mérens was regarded as a pony until 1998, when it was reclassified as a horse.

The head is large yet delicate in appearance, with small ears and wide-set eyes and nostrils. The neck can be on the short side, but the horse has a good sloping shoulder and an ample wither, a medium-to-long back and a strong round croup. The tail is low set, and the legs are of solid bone, but light and slightly short in comparison with the robust size of the body.

The Mérens not only has a quiet, gentle nature but is also outstandingly resistant to disease and can survive even when food is scarce.

LEFT *Noble and classically beautiful, the Mérens, as it is when living in the wild, is a true fairy-tale horse.*

A Pyrenean native

The lineage of the Mérens horse can be traced back to prehistoric times. Similar horses, with a dark coat, stocky build, an upright mane and tell-tale 'beard', are depicted on cave paintings at Niaux that date back some 13,000 years. The Magdalénian ancestors of the Mérens lived around the area of Tarascom-Sur-Ariège, thriving in relative isolation.

This small Pyrenean native is also the horse that Julius Caesar described in his commentaries on the Gallic War, written in the first century AD, as 'more tame than fast'. Seeing how these small, hardy horses could benefit their own horses, the Romans captured and tamed them in order to cross them with their hot-blooded horses of the East.

Life in the mountains

Over the centuries, the Mérens (also known as the Ariègeois) developed into a hardy, nimble and surefooted animal, perfectly adapted to life in the unforgiving Pyrenees.

Its robustness did not go unnoticed by the early farmers, known as the *montagnol*, who used Mérens horses on their mountain farms, where their ability to work over rocky ground and steep hills made them indispensable.

Mérens horses also served as army mounts, going into battle with the Count of Foix Gaston Phoebus in the Middle Ages – and even with Napoleon Bonaparte during his invasion of Russia. Their tractable nature, coupled with their minimal upkeep, made them ideal for cavalry support.

BELOW *Breed enthusiasts still insist that the only true Mérens is a horse raised free in the Pyrenees.*

ABOVE *Young Mérens are moved up to summer pastures to grow strong in the mountains.*

Throughout the years, the Mérens has continued to enjoy its relationship with the *montagnol*, ploughing the fields during the day and, under harness, driving the family into the local village at weekends. Its solid build and hardy, powerful nature meant the Mérens found many uses as a work horse: carrying packs, pulling farmer's wagons, shouldering supplies to the villages, tilling fields, transporting wood and working under saddle or in harness. Its quiet and gentle nature also made it an ideal horse for children, who could ride it with confidence. However, like most horse breeds, the Mérens faced an uncertain future when farming started to become more mechanized. Inevitably, by the turn of the century, the breed's numbers had fallen significantly.

The plight of the Mérens

Concerned individuals saw the plight of the Mérens and began selectively breeding the horse in around 1908. Breeders selected the most beautiful and conformationally correct horses to carry on the genes. In 1933, a society for the selection and promotion of the race, SHERPA (the *Syndicat Hippique d'Elevage de La Race Pyrenéenne Arièegeoise*) was created. The Mérens studbook was opened in 1947 and, through the aggressive activities of impassioned lovers of the breed, the Mérens numbers began to bounce back.

By 1970, there were less than 50 Mérens horses of breeding age. However, thanks to the diligent efforts of breeders, this number rose to 800 by 1980. In 1997, the SHERPA gave the then British Prime Minister Tony Blair a Mérens because of his affection for the Ariège area of France.

Although the Mérens as a breed is still rare, some breeders have established operations throughout France and even in other parts of Europe. However, many fans of the breed still insist that the conditions under which the Mérens is raised help to shape its character and endurance, so that the only true Mérens is a horse raised free in the Pyrenees.

The Mérens horse today

The relationship of the Mérens with the mountains continues. Breeders keep the horses in freedom, only gathering them when necessary. Each spring, foals are born on the mountainside, without any human interference. The breeders then move the herds up to summer pastures, where they can grow strong and nimble. Yet, unlike many horses that have little human contact, the Mérens is neither timid nor wary of people. When brought down off the mountains, the pony is easily trained and willing to work.

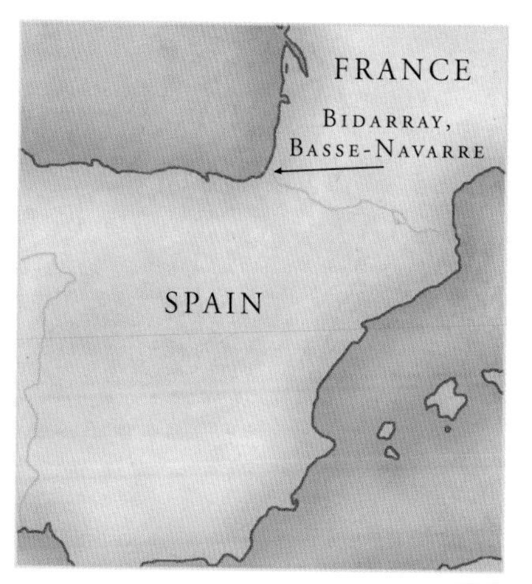

POTTOK *pony*

FRANCE AND SPAIN'S DARK MOUNTAIN-DWELLER

The Pottok (pronounced *pot-tee-ok*) gets its name from the Basque word *pottoka*, meaning 'little horse', and has been around for thousands of years. This ancient breed of pony has its home in the Basque region of south-western France and northern Spain, although some say that it may have descendants on the other side of the Atlantic Ocean, in the US.

The 'little horse'

The Pottok is a well put together horse-like pony with a pretty look about it. Its head has a straight profile, with small ears, large, intelligent eyes and wide nostrils. It has an upright, short neck, straight back, well-defined withers, well-sprung ribs and a sloping croup.

The ponies usually stand at about 12–13 hands (122–132 cm/48–132 in) and have medium-set tails and thick, bushy manes. While, hundreds of years ago, Pottoks were generally dark and solid-coloured, today most are coloured (piebald or skewbald).

Home in the Basque Country

The region known as the Basque Country lies in the western Pyrenees, partly in northern Spain and partly in south-western France, and stretching along the coast of the Bay of Biscay.

LEFT *Pottok ponies are said to be descendants of the Magdalénian horses of 14,000–7,000* BCE, *and even related to the now-extinct tarpan.*

ABOVE *Colourful Pottok ponies dot the Basque landscape, including those with piebald (black and white) coats.*

The Pottok pony may well have lived here since prehistoric times, since paintings found on cave walls throughout the area depict similar-looking horses. The Pottok is thought to be a descendant of the Magdalénian horses of 14,000–7,000 BC, and is believed to be a relative of the extinct tarpan. Over the centuries, this pony became perfectly adapted to its mountain home. Although small, it is nimble and hardy, and thrived in the rugged countryside. The altitude gave it excellent endurance, and its feet and legs became extremely tough from traversing the difficult terrain.

Some Pottok ponies were used for smuggling goods between France and Spain; because of their surefootedness and their dark coats, which camouflaged them at night, they were an ideal smuggler's horse. Other Pottoks found more legitimate roles, hauling wagons in the coalmines of Italy and northern France in the 19th and 20th centuries.

Although many of the Pottok ponies are brown or black, it is not unusual for colourful, flashy piebald horses to show up in the herd. As a result, some breed enthusiasts believe that it was the Pottok pony that gave rise to the often coloured horses of Assateague and Chincoteague islands, after being transported there by the Spanish (see Chincoteague pony, pages 32–37).

Most Pottok ponies remained free in the Basque Mountains of northern Spain – at least until recent history. While there were once thousands of Pottok ponies, there are now only a few hundred. This is due partly to habitat loss at the beginning of the 20th century and partly to cross-breeding, which has resulted in less hardy horses and fewer purebreds.

ABOVE *Like other European native ponies, Pottok ponies all have owners.*

BELOW *In spring, Pottock mares head to the higher pastures to foal in solitude.*

The piebald ponies were sought after as children's horses, so they were bred for colour. In addition, Spanish horses were introduced to make a larger sportier horse and draught horses were used to create a hybrid work horse. The Pottok in its pure form began to disappear at an alarming rate and, by the late 20th century, there were fewer than a couple of hundred purebred mares left.

The Pottok today

The Pottok pony was recognized by the French government in 1970, when an official studbook was created. While the ponies currently live in a semi-feral condition, they all have owners. A reserve in Bidarray, a small village at the base of the Pyrenees in the former Basque province of Basse-Navarre, was created to protect the pony and its native environment.

While there is great hope that the Pottok will increase in numbers, many individuals disagree about how this should take place – whether just to allow the purebred ponies to breed, or to use selective interbreeding to produce greater numbers of Pottok-like ponies quickly.

Traditionally Pottoks are gathered from the Pyrenees on the last Wednesday of January, branded for identification, and either sold or returned to the mountains that they have called home for centuries to live wild and, hopefully, prosper.

Galician *pony*

A Spanish treasure

This shy, wary pony lives in the mountains of Galicia. It is an ancient breed, related to a number of other European horses. It also plays an important role in the traditional Galician festival known as the 'Capture of the Beasts', which takes place each summer throughout the province and has become a major tourist attraction.

Galician home

Galicia is known in north-western Spain as the 'land of the thousand rivers'. These rivers criss-cross throughout the region, flowing from the mountainous inland to the coast, where they form the characteristic drowned river valleys known as *rias*. The coast itself offers great contrasts, from the smooth beaches of *Las Mariñas* to the dangerous cliffs of *Costa de la Muerte* – the 'coast of death'.

The climate is generally mild all year round, with reasonably warm, yet very wet winters and hot, slightly humid summers.

This is the home of the Galician pony, also called *Faca Galizana*, *Jaca gallega* and *Poney gallego* or *Poni galaga.*

The nature of the beast

LEFT *The original use of the Galician was to provide mane-and-tail hairs for brushes, but it was also used for its meat.*

Galician ponies are attractive, stout and strong-legged little equines, standing at 12–13 hands (122–132 cm/48–52 in). They have straight profiles, close-coupled bodies and short legs, and they are mostly chestnut or bay.

ABOVE *During* La Rapa das Bestas, *or 'The Capture of the Beasts', horses are rounded up, their manes cut, and tamed as part of a big festival.*

An interesting characteristic of one of the three types of Galician pony is the long moustache that appears on the upper lip of older mares.

A brief history

In 1973, a survey counted more than 20,000 ponies in Galicia, but the number today is much lower. This rugged, hardy pony is related to several European ponies. It has its origins with the ancient Celtic ponies, Roman horses and the horses imported into Spain by the Suebi, who invaded Spain in the 5th century. Some believe that the pony developed partly from the Garrano pony of Portugal. Over the years, other breeds have been introduced and bred with the Galician, resulting in today's large pony, or smallish horse.

Originally, the main use of the pony was to provide hair, from the mane and tail, for brush-making, although it was also used as a source of meat. A studbook was formed in 1994.

'The Capture of the Beasts'

Galician ponies play an important role in a fantastic event. One of the most traditional and popular festivals in Galicia is *La Rapa das Bestas*, or 'The Capture of the Beasts'. Galicians have been involved in taming *bestas* (beasts) since the Bronze Age and, even today, they continue to closely guard all the secrets surrounding a tradition which unfolds all over Galicia throughout the summer.

Apart from the local people, only well-informed travellers and horse-breeders usually have the privilege of seeing a group of feral ponies galloping at full speed in the Galician sierra. However, tourists can see this for themselves every weekend from June to August, as cities and villages hold their own *Rapa das Bestas.* This ancient rite that has now become a big attraction in the province. The day before the big event, the owners take all the ponies that they have rounded up to the *curro*, a traditional corral where the ponies are divided into groups. These *curros* are hidden away in the mountains of north and central Galicia, and scattered among the massifs close to the coast of La Coruña and Pontevedra.

On the day of the festival, once the action gets underway, the most expert horsemen, known as *agarradores* ('someone who seizes'), struggle with each of the horses in turn until they are able to control it sufficiently to brand it and cut off its mane. Once the skirmishes are over, a huge fiesta begins, to celebrate the taming of the animals.

ABOVE *Galician ponies are able to gain nourishment from the most unappetizing forage.*

BELOW *Many breeds have been introduced to the Galician herds, which has shaped this breed to what it is today.*

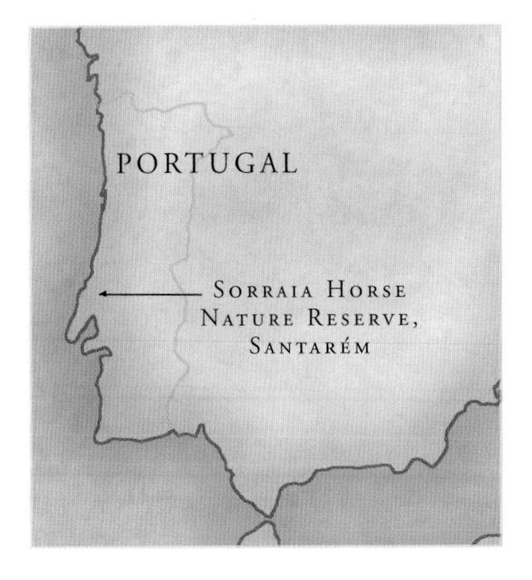

Sorraia *horse*

The fountainhead of Iberian horses

Many people are familiar with cave paintings of horses in France, but there are similar paintings on cave walls at La Pileta, in Spain, dating from between 30,000 and 20,000 BC. Unlike the French paintings, these depict horses with arched, crested necks which resemble the Sorraia, one of the most important feral horses in the world.

A horse from the past

The Sorraia still looks very like its primitive ancestors. It has a narrow, slightly convex head, tapering to a fine muzzle, with close-set, narrow eyes. It has an elegant, slightly crested neck, a refined throatlatch and the ability to flex gracefully downwards from the poll (the top of the head). The chest is narrow but deep, and the withers are prominent. The front end is elevated, the back is of medium length and the croup slopes gently, with a medium-set tail. The clean legs have rounded cannon bones and well-formed hooves.

Most Sorraias are no taller than 14.2 hands (147.5 cm/58 in) but those bred in captivity grow larger because they are better fed.

The coat of the Sorraia is a uniform mouse-dun (grulla) or yellow dun (regular dun), which seems to have been its coat colour through the ages. The horses have dark faces and muzzles, dark legs and dorsal stripes down the spine. They sport two-toned manes, with light outer hairs and dark hairs towards the inside. The ears are dark, but have light fluffy hair inside. The horses develop thick insulating coats during the winter.

LEFT *Although the Sorraia is not considered truly wild, this horse shares more features with ancient wild equines than most others.*

ABOVE *Horses are not solitary creatures; they desire the company of their own kind and Sorraia horses are no different.*

Their primitive markings are also often apparent, ranging from zebra stripes on the hocks and the backs of the legs to stripes across the shoulders, saw-tooth markings on the back, and even rump stripes. The stripes often fade with age and, as the breed is diluted through cross-breeding, these primitive markings disappear altogether.

Pure of race

Although the Sorraia is considered a free-roaming equine and not truly wild in a zoological sense, this horse still shares more features with ancient wild horses than nearly any other breed of horse. Found in the south of the Iberian Peninsula, they are the last remnant of the native Iberian horse and are directly related to the extinct tarpan.

The Sorraia was thought to be the well-spring of the *pura raza* (or 'pure race') horses – the Andalusian and the Lusitano – as well as the Spanish mustangs of the US and many other breeds. In fact, recent DNA analysis seems to confirm that American mustangs have similar DNA patterns to that of the Sorraia (see page 132).

The Sorraia is a prime example of a Spanish horse or, more accurately, an Iberian horse. There are other horses of Iberian type, but they often have blood of the Garrano – a pony that lived to the north of the Sorraia's habitat.

At some time in the past, the Sorraia probably also had a link with the North African Barb, via the prehistoric landbridge at Gibraltar.

Horses of the marsh

The native horse of the Iberian Peninsula was originally called the Marismeño, or 'horse of the marsh'. These wild horses, driven by encroaching civilization, had been forced to find a home on the swampy floodplains of the rivers. This fairly inaccessible wilderness enabled them to live in complete isolation from people.

Palaeontologist Ruy d'Andrade, who was also a breeder of Lusitano and Alter-Real horses, came upon the last remaining Marismeños – about 30 in all – on a hunting trip in Portugal in 1920. He found them near the mouth of the Sorraia River and therefore named them after that river. His interest now aroused, d'Andrade spent countless hours documenting these horses carefully. He was amazed to discover that this ancestral type of wild horse still existed, given that the numbers of Przewalski horses, another type of primitive wild horse, (see pages 160–167) in Mongolia were so few and the tarpan was extinct. His findings then led him to conclude that the *pura raza* horses were significantly influenced by this native horse.

BELOW *Research has shown that the Sorraia is very closely linked genetically to the now extinct tarpan.*

ABOVE *It is easy to see how the Sorraia has influenced the 'pure Spanish' horses' upright carriage, necks and profiles.*

He took a selection of the horses – reportedly 7 mares and 4 stallions – to breed on his estate. For the most part, the horses were left alone to breed on the pastures, although d'Andrade occasionally dictated which horses were placed together. Left to fend for themselves on d'Andrade's vast property, the mares bore foals and the numbers of horses grew, yet they still remained true to type. Because of the small gene pool, there was inevitably some inbreeding over the generations, which would have had serious consequences for typical domestic horse breeds. However, it did not seem to have any negative effects on the Sorraia.

New findings

A new study currently being conducted by German horse expert Hardy Oelke has so far produced some controversial preliminary findings. Oelke has shown through mitochondrial DNA testing that, while some strains of the American mustang indeed have the same DNA as the Sorraia, this DNA may not be present in the Andalusian and Lusitano. The study thus produced the unequivocal conclusion that the Sorraia horse that d'Andrade selected to study and preserve all those years ago is truly unique.

Oelke also determined that the Sorraia was completely different from the Garrano, the other Iberian primitive pony. The link with the Andalusian and Lusitano was seen clearly in the Sorraia's conformation, but the Garrano was much more like the ancient Celtic pony, being small, brown, with an often concave profile. Although small in height, the Sorraia's conformation was definitely horse-like, rather than pony-like. The teeth were also very different from those of the Garrano, although they showed many similarities to the teeth of the Andalusian.

The Sorraia has also influenced the signature elements of the *pura raza* horses, from its uphill conformation, arched neck and ability to break at the poll, to the way it carries itself, rounds its back and pushes from behind. It is also gaited and has influenced some of the Spanish horses that have lateral gaits. It is even known for adding a cattle-driving instinct to its descendants. In fact, it is courage that has allowed the Sorraia, and its supposed Iberian descendents – the Andalusian and Lusitano, to work with the bulls destined for fighting in the arena.

The Sorraia today

The Sorraia horses are no longer truly wild; instead they live mainly on the Sorraia Horse Nature Reserve, near Santarém in Portugal, which is owned by the Portuguese government and the heirs to the d'Andrade estate. José Luis Sommer d'Andrade carries on his grandfather's work by managing the horses and the large family estate while also working as the president of the Sorraia breed association.

There are only about 200 Sorraia horses left in the whole of Europe, although foals are still being born each spring. Nevertheless, with numbers this low, any breed would be in danger or extinction. The biggest challenge for the breed is that no stallions are being exchanged between the breeding groups on the studs, thus intensifying the already incredibly strong inbreeding. Another challenge is that the breeding horses chosen to continue the lineage may not be of the ideal type. Some breeders are biased when it comes to deciding which stallions to geld, and they may, for example, select horses that are more of a Lusitano type than of a Sorraia type.

BELOW *Most Sorraias live on the Nature Reserve in the Guadalquivir delta, rather than roaming free.*

ASTURIAN *pony*

SPANISH PONY WITH A UNIQUE GAIT

The unique feature of this pony is its ambling gait. Instead of moving its legs in diagonal fashion, like a trotting horse, it moves them in parallel – a characteristic that was probably inherited from its Celtic pony ancestors. As a result, ladies of old prized this little pony because it was so comfortable to ride side-saddle.

A pony of distinction

The Asturian is undoubtedly pony-sized, standing at 11.2–12.2 hands (117–127cm/46–50 in). The head, often thought of as medium in size, is often coarse in appearance, with a straight or sometimes convex profile and a large muzzle. The ears are small and foxy, the nostrils are large, and the large dark eyes sit prominently in the skull. Although on the short side, the neck is generally in proportion to the body; stallions tend to develop an arched crest.

The Asturian pony is fairly broad in the chest, well muscled over the body and have sturdy bone in the joints and legs. Its hooves are tough, the tail is fairly low set, and both mane and tail are thick and flowing. Most have dark coats: black or bay, or brown with no white.

Seaside home

LEFT *Romans were among the first to appreciate the gifts of the Asturian pony.*

Asturias, a coastal principality in northern Spain, is bordered by the Cantabrian Sea to the north, Galicia to the west, Cantabria to the east, and

ABOVE *Asturian ponies are adept at finding shelter among the rocky outcroppings and trees of their home.*

Castile and Leon to the south. It is an area of many contrasts: on one side there is a breathtaking coastline, with sheer cliff faces that protect its beautiful beaches and azure waters; on the other, the rugged Cantabrian mountain range forms a natural border between Asturias and Castile and Leon. The rivers are short yet abundant sources of water, fed throughout the year by the heavy rainfall and, in late spring, by melting snow from the mountains. Winters can be cold while summers can be humid.

The Asturian ponies, or *Asturcones*, are thought to have existed here for 3,000 years and, despite once being in grave danger of extinction, they are currently aided by groups that are helping them in their fight for survival.

Ancient origins

The Asturian pony is an ancient breed, and devout breed enthusiasts argue that it is one of the oldest and purest of equines. Even so, its origins are shrouded in mystery. Some people believe that its ancestry lies with the

Iberian Sorraia (see page 132), the Spanish Garrano and the extinct Celtic pony. A few ancient texts note that the Romans took some of these small horses for use by their troops in the service of the Roman Empire.

Whatever its origins, the little Asturian pony has remained a distinct type of equine over the centuries, and today is one of the few native horses found in southern Europe. It has not changed much in the last 2,800 years.

The Asturian pony also played a key role in the economics of Spain. In the 15th century, because of their sturdy nature and hardy constitution, they were exported to Ireland, where they were interbred with Irish stock and helped to develop the Irish Hobby horse. They were also exported to Paris, where they were used as small cart horses and became known as *haubini* horses and, later, as *hobbye* horses. In England, they were called palfreys. In their native Spain, herds were sold off to various regions for use in farming.

ABOVE *Asturians are predominantly black or bay with no white markings.*

BELOW *The Asturian has faced near extinction, but recently activist groups have been formed to protect the pony.*

The Asturian pony today

In Asturia the ponies are now registered and branded. The Association of Criadores de Ponis de Raza Asturcón, founded in 1981, is charged with updating the studbook. It keeps a record of every colt born in each year and issues a corresponding certificate (Genealogical Letter).

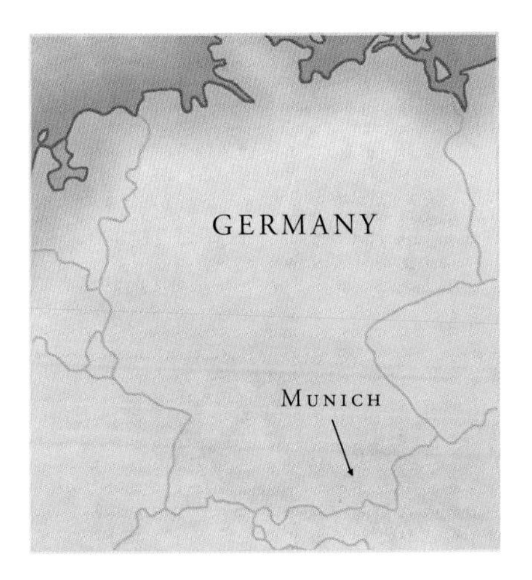

HECK *horse*

A PRODUCT OF GERMAN ENGINEERING

The Heck horse is the product of selective breeding between the truly wild Przewalski horse (see pages 160–167) and various domestic horse breeds chosen for their relationship to the recently extinct tarpan. It resulted from an attempt by two German zoologists, Lutz and Heinz Heck, to substantiate their theory that extinct animals, in this case the tarpan, could be re-created.

The tarpan

The tarpan (or Eurasian wild horse) was first described in 1774, by the German naturalist Johann Friedrich Gmelin, who observed the horse in its home region of Bobrovsk. He considered it to be a separate species from the domestic horse (*Equus caballus*) and gave it the specific name *Equus ferus*.

It was still in existence during the last Ice Age and, as cave paintings show, it was hunted for food by Stone-Age peoples. However, the tarpan always shared a tumultuous relationship with man, as many were destroyed when civilization expanded, because people didn't want the wild horses breeding with their domestic ones. The last herds vanished in the 20th century, after ranging eastwards into the Ukrainian steppes of the Ukraine. It finally became extinct in 1918, when the last captive specimen died in the Ukraine.

Therefore, despite the abundance of many breeds of feral horses living throughout the whole world, the only truly wild horse still in existence is the Przewalski horse.

LEFT *The modern Tarpan, or Heck horse, is a genetic recreation of the original wild breed.*

Above *The first Heck horse, considered the first back-crossed tarpan, was born on 22 May 1933 at the Tierpark Hellabrunn in Munich.*

Echoes of the past

Although the tarpan is now extinct, some traces of its original gene pool remain, like fingerprints, in a number of crossbred domestic horses. Polish farmers crossed their native horses with the tarpan, producing the *konik* (or 'small horse'), a term applied to a number of Central European breeds in which tarpan DNA can be found. The *koniks* display many primitive features; for example, one breed, the Bilgoraj konik, has a dun coat and a dorsal stripe.

In the 1930s, Lutz Heck, Director of the Berlin zoo, and his brother Heinz Heck, who was working at the Munich zoo, developed a theory that all living creatures were a result of their gene combinations and that, by reassembling their genes, extinct animals could be re-created. The only drawback was finding an extinct animal that had living descendants, which is why they chose the tarpan for their experiments.

Bringing back the extinct tarpan

The Heck brothers decided to re-create the tarpan by a process of back-crossing (or *Rückzüchtung*), using captive Przewalski stallions and mares of the *koniks*, the Icelandic pony, Gotland pony and the primitive horses living in the Polish reserve of Bialowieza. These mares were similar in build and skull shape to the tarpan.

The Przewalski horse is quite different from the tarpan, so the Heck brothers used it very carefully in their breeding programme. The tarpan was small, but fine-boned, with delicate features, a mouse-grey coat and zebra-striped legs; the Przewalski horse is meatier, more compact and more robust.

The mares were mated with the Przewalski stallions in the hope that the wild blood would bring out the characteristics of the tarpan lying dormant in these more modern breeds. Initially, the foals that were produced had too many of the coarse traits of the Przewalski horse. Then, an occasional mouse-grey foal would be born, which was interesting because none of the original mares had grey coats. Foals with a profile more like the Przewalski were taken out of the breeding programme. Gradually, after careful selection of horses with the most appropriate traits, the Heck horse, the first back-crossed tarpan, was born on 22 May 1933 at the Tierpark Hellabrunn in Munich. Soon there was a herd of Heck horses at the zoo.

The Heck brothers also developed a version of the aurochs, the wild, bison-like ancestor of modern cattle. Neither the Heck aurochs nor the Heck horse have any domestic value, but both have shown an unusual resistance to disease. 'The day may come', noted Dr Heck, 'when our highly bred, highly strung modern breeds will need a shot of their wild ancestors' blood to revitalize them'.

ABOVE *The konik and the Przewalski helped shape the Heck breeding program.*

BELOW *The Heck horse lacks the bristly upright mane of the tarpan.*

The result

Although the Heck horse is similar to the original tarpan in its skeletal conformation and mousey coat, there is no genetic evidence to show that it is really identical. One characteristic of the true tarpan that the Heck brothers could not recreate is the upright mane. However, Heck horses are all quite uniform in size, conformation and colour, more so than many of their feral brethren.

The Heck horse also has other traits of the tarpan. It seems to be resistant to harsh weather and can exist on poor forage, as well as having high fertility and an excellent ability to carry foals to term. It also has a robust immune system and can fend off infection better than domestic horses.

When newborn, Heck foals are wheat-brown. When they become weanlings their coats begin to turn grey and zebra stripes appear on their legs.

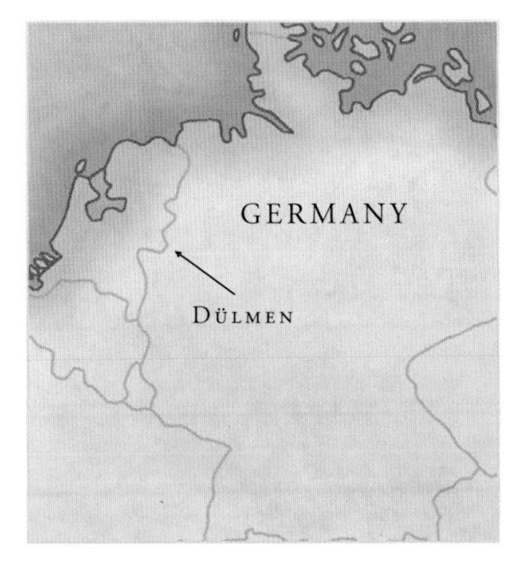

DÜLMEN *pony*

THE LAST OF GERMANY'S NATIVE BREEDS

Germany is famed for its warm-bloods and is home to some of the finest sport horses ever bred for competition, whether for show-jumping, dressage or combined training. These equine athletes may be renowned for their success in Olympic disciplines, but they are not as unique as the small feral pony, called the Dülmen, which may have contributed to its larger cousins.

Primitive appearance

Small, close-coupled and sturdy, the Dülmen pony has a primitive appearance. It has a small pony-type head, a short neck, lightly boned legs and a short back. It can be round in the barrel, with little wither, and usually stands at 12–13 hands (122–132 cm/48–52 in). Most ponies are a mousy-dun colour with black points, although some that are not purebred can be dark bay, brown, chestnut or even black.

Lordly intervention

LEFT *Dülmens live on a nature reserve known as Wildpferdebahn Merfelder Bruch, in Germany.*

The Dülmen pony (or Dülmener) is the last of Germany's native breeds. Records of this pony date back as far back as 1316, when herds of wild, mouse-coloured horses were documented as living in an area called Merfelder Bruch, near Dülmen, in north-western Germany. Only the most robust and smartest survived the severe winters, which eventually resulted in

Above *Each year the ponies are rounded up, with excess Dülmen colts removed for sale.*

a very hardy, enduring little pony. This hilly meadow and woodland, situated in Westphalia (now North Rhine-Westphalia) has been the home of these ponies for 700 years, with small herds thriving in different pockets of the common land, although they were often mistreated and victimized.

At that time, the Lord of Melfeld was given the rights over this region and over the herd of ponies. On his land, the ponies finally found refuge and survived the centuries, the harsh winters and humid summers – watched over by the lord of the manor and the nearby farmers who shared the common land. It is said that breeders took the Dülmen and crossed it with other breeds to create the Hanoverian warm-blood.

In the 1800s, when the common land was divided and the burgeoning villages and towns started to encroach on the countryside, the areas available for the feral ponies shrank. Even the Merfelder Bruch was no longer a haven. In about 1840, the Dukes of Croy became the landowners of a portion of Merfeld, and they inherited the last remaining ponies, which numbered about 20, along with the estate.

They set aside a sanctuary for the ponies, covering 3.5 km^2 (1.5 sq. miles, or 860 acres), where the ponies could live in relative isolation and safety. Despite being under human jurisdiction, the ponies still relied only on their instinct and cunning to survive. Even so, within the following decades their numbers grew from a scant handful to more than 350, although other breeds of horse and ponies were released into the herd, including British native ponies and some Polish horses.

ABOVE *Dorsal striping can be seen not only running down the length of spine, but also into the tail.*

BELOW *Near black, flint-hard hooves are a recognizable trademark of the Dülmen.*

The future

Today, the nature reserve known as Wildpferdebahn Merfelder Bruch allows the Dülmen pony to carry on as it has for previous centuries: finding its own food and shelter, and coping with the cycle of life – breeding, foaling and death. Two key missions of the reserve, which is owned by the Duke of Croy, are to keep the breed pure by preventing further cross-breeding, and to preserve the area in which the ponies live, because this is essential to keeping the breed character consistent. Due to the isolation of the Dülmen ponies, geneticists are particularly interested in seeing how their behaviour in the wild differs from that of domestic horses, even though they are not classified as wild.

Each year, on the last Saturday of May, the ponies are rounded up for inspection. The colts are then separated and sold at a public auction, while the mares are returned with only one or two stallions. The Dülmen is a good riding pony and, despite its wild origins, is smart and willing, and is even good pulling a cart or working on a farm.

With human support, the Dülmen pony has a brighter future than many other wild horses. It is only because of the legacy of the Dukes of Croy, and their benevolence toward the Dülmen pony over the centuries, that this national treasure has been allowed to thrive.

Giara *pony*

Roman pony of the island

This small pony roams the island of Sardinia, and today it is one of the last of its kind in the region. Dating from the pre-Roman period, this diminutive equine originally flourished all over the Giara plateau, living a half-wild existence: rounded up in May, the mares would work through the harvesting season before being returned to the wild until the following year.

Seasonal work

The Giara ponies are longstanding inhabitants of the island. Although their exact origins are unclear, most are agreed that their arrival predates the Roman period, and many believe that the Carthaginians may have brought *Cavallino della Giara*, or the Giara Pony, over from Numidia with them.

Over the centuries, the ponies have lived a half-wild existence. During medieval times, mares would be captured and used for threshing chores. They would be used for the whole of the harvesting season in the nearby plains of the Campidano, but they would then be returned to the wild on the Giara plateau, to once again live free for the remainder of the year.

But even the island of Sardinia eventually developed mechanized farming methods and the ponies lost their usefulness. As their work disappeared, numbers began to dwindle. Many of the ponies were slaughtered for their meat. An attempt to boost the equine population took place in the mid-1900s, when larger stallions were set free with the Giara herd. While the aim

Left *Giara ponies are mostly found on the Altopiano della Giara plateau, about 70 km (45 miles) from the town of Oristano, on the island of Sardinia.*

to give the ponies a little more size and substance was well-meant, many lovers of the breed were appalled to see that the Giara characteristics were beginning to vanish, and traits such as white patches and light manes and tails started cropping up in the new horses. In the 1970s, a movement to keep the ponies' bloodlines pure began, and any horses bearing uncharacteristic features were removed from the herd.

Island isolation

The Giara of Gesturi's natural isolation not only shaped the pony into what it is today, but also helped to preserve the breed's characteristics, as did their environment. The plateau is home to many *paulis*, marshes of varying sizes formed by rainwater that pools and stagnates in wide, ancient volcanic hollows. Enduring the hot, humid or windy weather, and poor shelter among the *paulis*, the ponies stayed small but hardy. They broke into smaller herds of 20 mares and foals, guarded by one stallion. Colts, once matured, were kicked out of the band by the elder stallion to seek their own herd.

The Giara ponies, which number about 500 at any one time, are small – standing only 12.2 hands high (127 cm/50 in) – and stocky. Purebreds are dark (either brown, black or bay), sporting lush manes and tails, short upright necks and straight profiles, square heads and full jowls. They have small foxy ears and large almond-shaped eyes. They possess low withers, powerful croups and slender legs with hard hooves. Like most feral horses, they are cautious, timid and will take flight easily if startled. However, they can and have been in the past successfully tamed to be saddle ponies.

BELOW *The breed is known locally as* Cavallino della Giara.

Modern island living

Today, the ponies are mostly found on the Altopiano della Giara plateau, 600 m (1,969 ft) above sea level, about 70 km (45 miles) from the town of Oristano. In order to both keep track of the ponies and protect the bloodlines of the equines, all of them are taken from the plateaus in roundups each year in August. This is also done for the ponies' nutritional benefit, as during the hottest months of the year the forage becomes rather scarce. They are placed in stone-walled holding paddocks which have been used year after year. The herd is looked over and then separated into groups for branding. There are three different brands the pony receives to signify the Giara pony breed: its purity, its owner (usually families in nearby villages) and the area it is from. The ponies deemed pure Giara blood receive a G brand, while those that are not receive an R and are not returned to the wild, but are sold to nearby villages.

The branding is a culmination of a small festival and horse race called *is insocadores*. Later, in September, the pure Giara ponies are returned to run wild for another year. Since 1996 a group called the 25th Mountain Community has been purchasing Giara ponies from local villagers and can now lay claim to more than a third of the ponies that live on the island.

Today tourism also promotes the island ponies as a point of interest among the other flora and fauna. Visitors often hike out or mountain bike to the plateau to see the ponies in their habitat. The ponies again are assisting the local economy – not with their muscle this time, but with their wild existence that tourists find so appealing.

ABOVE *Since Medieval times these ponies were used for threshing.*

BELOW *Their presence in Sardinia probably dates from pre-Roman times.*

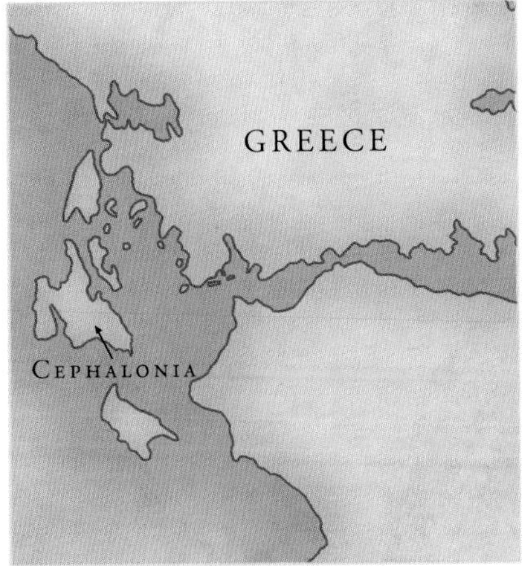

CEPHALONIA *pony*

PREVENTING A GREEK TRAGEDY

The pine forests of Mount Ainos, in Cephalonia, are home to fewer than two dozen of these wild ponies. These tough, resilient animals are the descendants of horses that were captured in mainland Greece and sold to the islanders. One of the few feral horse herds in Greece, they are said to be direct descendants of Alexander the Great's horses.

Small but hardy

The Cephalonia pony is extremely shy and wary. While it is noted for its extreme hardiness and tremendous stamina, its hallmark is its surefootedness – the product of generations of adaptation to life in mountainous conditions and rough terrain that would break the legs of normal horses.

This is a small pony, standing at 10–12 hands (102–122 cm/40–48 in). Narrow through the barrel and chest, it has a straight profile, dark eyes, and a full mane and tail. It is dark in colour, varying from bay and grey-blue roan to mousey. They are extremely shy and wary.

Because there is no Greek word for 'pony', its name is also often translated into English as 'Cephalonia horse'.

Life on Mount Ainos

Cephalonia (or Kefalonia), the largest of the Ionian islands on the west of mainland Greece, benefits from its closeness to Italy and the rest of Europe. It is a green island, rich in vegetation, and in spring, the hills and fields come alive with colourful wildflowers. Mount Ainos is the third highest mountain

LEFT *Loss of woodland, along with culling by the local farmers, contributed to the pony's decline.*

ABOVE *The Cephalonia ponies originated from a hardy breed of horses native to mainland Greece.*

in Greece, and the Mount Ainos National Park, established in 1962, is noted for its unique Cephalonian pines.

The Cephalonia ponies originated from a hardy breed of horses native to the Arta region, just south of the Pindos Mountains in the north of mainland Greece. They were introduced to Cephalonia by the islanders, who bought them from mainland cattle fairs to use as work horses. Over the centuries, the wild herd grew as horses either escaped or were turned loose by their owners. The old custom of allowing horses to range free on the mountain in order to avoid the costs of feeding them added to their numbers. Most horses were abandoned permanently to the wild after World War II.

Since acquiring their freedom, these ponies have lived as one or two bands for a century, near the only spring on Mount Ainos. Although the area is forested, most of the terrain is rugged and extremely rocky, and the horses had to navigate deep ravines and gullies. However, to begin with, forage was plentiful enough to sustain the horses – and other native wildlife – through the rough winters.

Because of the remoteness of their habitat and their timid, wary nature, the horses spent years in complete isolation, but the survivors of the harsh winters, poor forage and poor water supply became hardier with each generation. As a result, over time, the Cephalonia pony was eventually classified as a distinct breed.

Hard times

Feral animals do not have an easy life in Greece, as most are regarded as pests that need to be eradicated. Many of the ponies were killed because the Cephalonian farmers believed that they were competing with their sheep and goats for forage. In addition, the pine forests were felled for timber or devastated by fires, forcing the ponies into ever more remote areas, where there was often no shelter to protect from the elements. As a result, their numbers shrank even more.

Plans for the future

Concerned islanders and former residents, united by their concern for the ponies, formed the Environmental League for the Animals in the Ionian (ELATI). Their plans include the establishment of a viewing centre where visitors can watch these shy horses, thereby increasing tourism in the remoter areas of the island. They also want to ensure that breeding continues unhindered so that the numbers of horses can stabilize. They also hope to improve the ponies' environment so that they have a better chance of long-term survival. This includes plans to set up feeding stations, to take the pressure of the farmers' grazing land and improving the paths used by the ponies in order to reduce the incidence of often serious injuries to their leg bones. The group believes that the ponies, in return, will contribute to the island's tourist economy and thus secure their existence in the future. They are an integral part of the environment of both public and national-park land and should be valued in the same way as other resources within the area.

BELOW *The Cephalonia herds are shy by nature, and can usually only be viewed from afar.*

SKYROS *pony*

GRECIAN SURVIVOR

Perhaps it is the hardiness of ponies that allows them to thrive, to beat the odds and live where others have perished. The pony of Skyros Island is desperately trying to survive, but not because its habitat is dwindling, or that it has to eke out an existence. In an ironic twist of fate, it is a law that could be the pony's undoing.

Island home

The Skyros (or Skyrian) pony is found on Skyros, the largest and most southerly island of the Sporades, lying to the east of mainland Greece in the Aegean Sea. The island consists of two different environments: the northern side is green and fertile, and ideal for agriculture, while the southern side is mountainous, rather treacherous and often dry in summer.

Horse or pony?

The Greek name for this pony is *Helliniko alogaki*, which can be translated as 'little Greek horse'. There is no Greek word for 'pony', so even though the Skyros pony is small in stature, its name is often translated into English as 'Skyros horse'.

The Skyros pony is very small, usually standing at only about 11 hands (122 cm/44 in), and is similar to the Exmoor pony (see pages 90–93), but in miniature. The ponies are dark brown or bay, with fawn muzzles and eye areas, a colouring often known as 'mealy'. Like the Exmoor, they have deep, hooded eyes (called a 'toad eye') that are wide-set and intelligent and small

LEFT *The Skyros Pony is by all accounts in danger of extinction, although no government or international authority has declared this yet.*

ABOVE *Genetically, the ponies can be traced back to prehistoric horses.*

heads with slightly convex profiles. Their necks are short but slender, chests are narrow, and the bodies are slender, with lightly muscled hindquarters. They have low-set tails and hard black hooves – any horse with light hooves is not a purebred Skyros pony.

Mysterious origins

Unlike many European horses that were crossed with North African Barb horses, the Skyros ponies remained true to their original type because they had no opportunity to breed with the Barb. Their isolation kept their gene pool pure.

It may have been Skyros ponies that Alexander the Great took with him when he left Macedonia to conquer the world. Some have also remarked on the similarity of the Skyros pony to the magnificent horses depicted on the Parthenon frieze, part of which (known as the Elgin Marbles) is housed in the British Museum. A comparison of the proportions of the horses and their riders suggests that they are truly small horses, rather than being reduced disproproportionately in size by the sculptor in order to emphasize the riders' stature.

Life on Skyros

Over the centuries, these ponies have had a good relationship with humans, being used on farms for harvesting grain and as riding ponies, pack ponies and cart ponies. They were also used as breeding partners for mules.

Their lives are a mixture of domesticity and wild living. They spend their winters alone on the southern mountain, where pasture is still good and water is available. In summer, however, the grasses dry up and disappear, and the ponies must look to the north for food and water. Farmers provided this and, in exchange, they used the ponies for threshing the grain crop.

In the 1950s, with advances in agricultural practices, threshing equipment arrived on the island, followed by cross-country vehicles and combine-harvesters. The pony that was once valued as a partner on the farm quickly became obsolete. Even worse for the ponies, the government gave grants to farmers for keeping sheep and goats, which had a dramatic effect on the grazing land. As a result, the numbers of Skyros ponies diminished.

Declining population

The first census of Skyros ponies, taken in 1993, showed a total population of 121 ponies. Moreover, a local law prohibited the export of any purebred

Skyros pony from the island. This was damaging in several ways because the law did permit the export of part-bred ponies. As a result, many farmers bred the ponies with donkeys to create mules and hinnies to sell on the mainland.

Concerned individuals started to take notice and organize to help the ponies. Silvia Dimitriadis Steen was approached in Corfu and asked to provide a home for four Skyros ponies: two stallions and two mares. So began the Silva Project in 1996, a refuge on the Silva estate, located on the Kanoni Peninsula near Corfu Town.

Another supporter was Alec Copeland, who was a member of the veterinary faculty at Edinburgh University, in Scotland. Copeland, who was very familiar with British native pony breeds and in particular the Exmoor pony, Britain's most ancient horse breed, took a keen interest in the Skyros pony. He visited the island to investigate the ponies himself and found that the Skyros pony was similar to the Exmoor in conformation, gait and temperament. It was just smaller.

In 2004, another census revealed that there were 90 ponies left on Skyros, of which only 14 were purebred.

Silva Project

The Silva Project is now working hard to change the law so that purebreds can be exported. This would enable Silva to set up breeding operations and pony refuges on the mainland. In addition, having ponies in other parts of the world improves its odds for survival; at the moment, if an outbreak of disease were to sweep the islands, the entire herd could be wiped out.

As a non-profit organization, the Silva Project is also trying to set up a herd book to help identify, track and maintain the ponies in the herd. Ponies are microchipped for identification, which helps with keeping track of individual ponies.

BELOW *Because there are so few ponies, inbreeding could further endanger the ponies' survival.*

The future

The studbook that was set up by the Silva Project for the Skyros ponies can help with more than just tracking the animals. As with the Exmoor, pony, setting a purebred standard can help to preserve the breed for the future, and impure traits such as white legs and white markings on the face can be phased out. With the assistance of Silva, Rare Breeds International and other similar organizations, it is hoped that farmers and breeders will turn to breeding purebred ponies and thus ensure the future of the *alogaki*.

ASIA

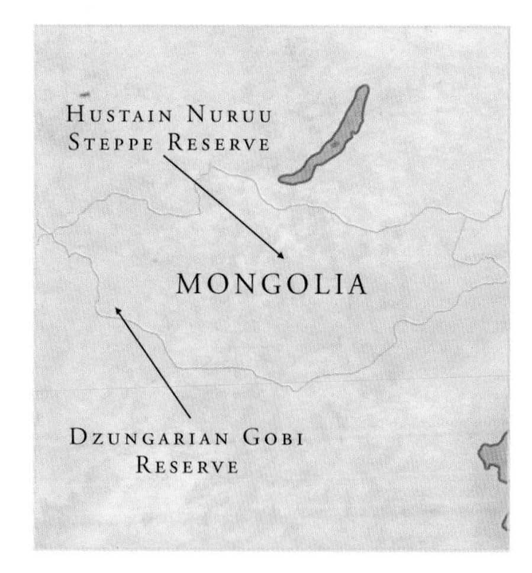

PRZEWALSKI *horse*

THE TRUE WILD HORSE

Of the millions of horses all over the world, nearly 200 are domestic breeds. And, amazingly, although the domestic cat and dog still have plenty of wild relatives, the horse can claim only one: the Przewalski horse, also known as the Asiatic wild horse, the *takhi* (meaning 'spirit' in Mongolian) and the *kertag*, as it called by the Kirghiz people.

Return from extinction

After the last Ice Age, 20,000 years ago, a primitive horse (*Equus ferus*) roamed in numerous herds throughout Europe and Asia. From cave paintings, zoologists learned that early humans used these equines mainly for meat and hides. It was not until much later, about 6,000 years ago, that they began to use them for transport rather than food. As a result, these primitive horses became domesticated. Those horses that remained in the wild were not welcome near homesteads. The stallions tended to steal domesticated mares, and bands of horses often broke into enclosures and destroyed the youngsters, so these wild horses were either hunted down or forced further into the wilderness.

Three primitive horses are considered to be the foundation of all domestic horses: the forest horse, the tarpan, and the Asiatic wild horse, which came from the steppes of northern Eurasia – a large semi-arid, grass-covered plain with scattered woods.

The Asiatic wild horse was considered extinct until the Russian cartographer Colonel Nikolai Mikhailovitch Przewalski (pronounced *pris-vaal-ski*) caught sight of a herd of dun-coloured horses while mapping the

LEFT *The milk of Przewalski mares is sometimes made into an elixir, which is drunk by native peoples.*

Tachin Schah Mountains in Mongolia in 1879. The native Kirghiz, who used the *kertag* for meat, gave Przewalski a skull and hide to take back to Russia to show the Tsar. Zoologists there were intrigued by these specimens and soon began to think that these horses were Asiatic wild horses.

Because this horse was considered extinct when Swedish scientist Linnaeus was developing his binomial naming system, the Asiatic wild horse was not included. Subsequently, the names of any new animals that were found included the name of their discoverer as well as the name of the person who first described them. Therefore, when zoologist J. S. Poliakov described the horse in 1881, it was named *Equus caballus przewalskii* Poliakov.

However, while Colonel Przewalski took the credit for discovering the horse, he was not the first to do so. As early as 1427, Hans Schiltberger, a Bavarian royal who was sold by the Turks to a Mongol prince, wrote of the horse in his memoirs, and, in 1719, a Scottish doctor, sent to China by Peter the Great, also wrote of the horse. An English naturalist, Colonel Hamilton Smith, who visited Mongolia in 1814, also talked about the wild horse and published his findings in Jardine's Naturalist's Library.

Built for survival

The Przewalski horse is said to be aggressive yet shy of humans. Horses raised in zoos may be wary but they are easily approached. They are tough horses that can go a long time without water and can exist on very meagre rations.

The Przewalski horse stands at 13–14 hands (132–142 cm/52–56 in), with a large head that bears a Roman nose, high-set eyes and a protruding profile. The mane stands up and ends between the ears, with no forelock. The conformation is very ass-like, with chunky features, such as short quarters, a straight back and no withers. The tail hairs start below the dock, much like those of a donkey. The Przewalski is mostly dun with black points, a cream stomach and a dorsal stripe, but sometimes also red dun with white markings.

Life in captivity

In the 1800s, the popular fashion for collecting spurred an interest in the horses. Zoological gardens had become popular, and so several wealthy men wanted to own rare animals and were prepared to go to great lengths to get them. One of these men, Friedrich von Falz-Fein from Ukraine, sent collectors in 1889 to capture a stallion and two mares. Not wishing to be left

LEFT *The Przewalski horse is said to have a bold nature, yet is naturally wary of humans.*

ABOVE *The Przewalski is different from other so-called wild horses, as it has 66 chromosomes instead of 64.*

out, the Duke of Bedford, who was chairman of the Zoological Society of London at the time, sent Carl Hagenback, a German animal collector, to bring him 17 colts and 15 fillies.

The Przewalski horses were not easy to catch. They were tough and could run for great distances over any type of ground and for a long periods of time. When in pursuit, the collectors often had to use three of their own horses, spaced at strategic intervals, so that they could change to a fresh horse whenever necessary. The foals of the wild horses could not keep up with the adults and would fall to the ground in exhaustion. The collectors would then sweep them up, bring them back to their base camp and put them to domestic in-milk mares.

Sadly, many of the foals died soon after capture or on the ship to their new home. In all, 51 were captured from the wild and sent to the US and to Europe, but only half of them survived. Ironically, they would later save the species from extinction.

Declining population

The population of Przewalski horses was fairly small in the wild, but growing, until World War II, when overhunting by the native Kirghiz threatened their survival. Their numbers dwindled until the final sighting of the last band of wild horses, at the Gun Tamga spring (now a nature reserve) on the border between China and Mongolia, in 1968. By the end of that year, the Przewalski horse was considered extinct in the wild.

Things were equally bad for the horses held in captivity. They were not breeding well because the zoos kept them in tiny enclosures with little grazing. Since there was no studbook or exchanges between zoos, breeding was very haphazard, with stallions often mating with their own daughters. In 1977, there were only 300 horses alive in captivity and only 13 of these were suitable for further breeding. Zoologists realized that the only way to preserve the species was to return them to the wild.

Return to Mongolia

Also in 1977, three scientists from the Netherlands set up the Foundation for the Preservation and Protection of the Przewalski Horse (FPPPH). Their goal was to set up a studbook and to help zoos understand how to breed the horses. They wanted to improve the poor breeding practice by encouraging zoos to exchange animals.

BELOW *Many get their first introduction to the Przewalski while visiting zoos.*

The FPPPH also wanted to consider setting the horses free in their native land, but how fair was it to turn zoo-reared animals into such a harsh environment? Weather in the steppes of Mongolia could be blisteringly hot at one moment and a howling blizzard at the next. Wolves could easily prey on any animal unused to being chased. The original Przewalski horse was adapted to deal with both climate and predators, but would captive-raised animals still have that native hardiness? The FPPPH was taking no chances and set up five semi-reserves in the Netherlands and Germany, so that the horses could learn to become wild again.

The FPPPH found that the horses best suited to re-introduction should be no more than 3 years of age, accustomed to weather fluctuations and capable of dealing with predators. They also had to be introduced in already-established groups.

In 1979, the Mongolian Vice President, who wanted to see the horses returned, began to work with the FPPPH. The Soviet government was suspicious of the re-introduction and stopped the first shipment of horses into China. In 1990, after the Iron Curtain had fallen, the Mongolian government tried again. They set aside two reserves to welcome their national symbol: the Dzungarian Gobi Reserve in the Gobi Desert and the Hustain Nuruu Steppe Reserve (made a national park in 1998) in central Mongolia. In 1994, four acclimatized breeding groups and one mixed group were released in the Hustain Nuruu reserve and three breeding groups and one bachelor group were released in the Gobi Reserve. As a result, 200 horses now run free in Mongolia.

Today, there are currently 1,500 Przewalski horses worldwide: 1,200 are in captivity (150 in North America) and 300 are running wild or acclimatizing. The FPPPH's goal is eventually to have the entire captive gene pool represented in the wild.

Past and present roles

It is rumoured that Ghengis Khan, conquerer of the civilized world, and his Mongol hordes were mounted on Przewalski horses but, apart from a picture of a Russian Cossack riding a Przewalski in the 1800s, shown in the book *The Asiatic Wild Horse* by Dr Erna Mohr, no one has ever trained a Przewalski horse.

Interestingly, the Przewalski horse differs from modern-day horses, in that it has 66 chromosomes instead of 64. If the Przewalski were crossed with a domestic horse, the resulting offspring would have 65 chromosomes. And if these offspring were crossed again with a domestic horse, the progeny would have the standard 64 chromosomes.

However, it does not matter whether the Przewalski horse is ever ridden, or if its bloodline is ever used to enhance domestic breeds. Its value as a crucial link to ancient times and a final glimpse into the past of present-day horses is inestimable.

LEFT *Horses that are ideal for re-introduction to their native land are no more than 3 years of age, accustomed to changeable weather and capable of fending off predators.*

AFRICA

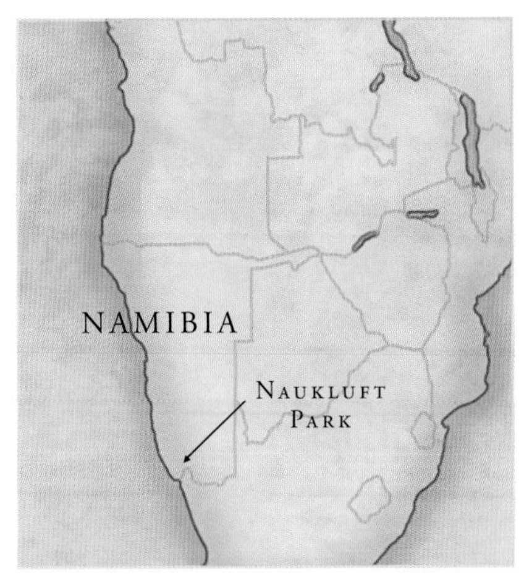

Namib *wild horse*

Surviving the impossible

Massive dunes stretch as far as the eye can see. The piercing blue sky is in sharp contrast to the ochre sands, where only the occasional lone shrub survives. Heat radiates from the desert floor; to draw a breath is to draw in furnace air. Dusk falls, and a small group of horses emerges, shuffling purposefully through the dunes.

African desert home

The Namib Desert, considered to be one of the oldest deserts in the world, has endured arid or semi-arid conditions for at least 55 million years. Although annual rainfall is limited to only 5–76 mm (0.2–3 in) and it is nearly completely barren, thick fog from the Atlantic often blankets the dunes, creating enough moisture for a handful of species to survive.

Carved from a brutal environment

The Namib wild horse is the product of these harsh desert conditions. Small and hardy, most are pony-sized, at about 14.2 hands (147.5 cm/58 in), although a few may reach 15 hands (152.5 cm/60 in).

While their conformation varies, they generally have large heads with convex profiles and small muzzles, large ears, wide-set eyes and short necks. They also have narrow chests, prominent withers and average-length legs, and are narrow through their girths, with sloping croups. Most horses are chestnut, although various bays and browns are also found.

Left *The Namib horses have learned to adapt to some of the most extreme desert conditions in the world.*

ABOVE *The Namib horse must often go without water for several days.*

Unlikely desert residents

Nobody knows exactly how the wild horses came to the desert. Originally there were no horses in southern Africa. They only started to appear in the region from the 17th century onwards, imported by Europeans. Most people regard the German occupation as the fountainhead. Some believe that the horses came from the former breeding operation of the eccentric Baron Hansheinrich von Wolf, who kept horses at his peculiar castle of Duwisib, south of Maltahöhe. Others say that German colonial forces left behind horses during World War I, as they retreated from the advancing South African troops.

There is also a rather far-fetched theory that a ship with a cargo of horses and other domestic animals was wrecked about 25 km (15 miles) south of the Orange River mouth, roughly 200 km (125 miles) from Garub, in the late 19th century. The horses that managed to escape then migrated far into the desert.

Drought and doubt

The population of Namib horses is currently about 150, and these horses attract thousands of tourists each year. The feral horses of the Namib live in Naukluft Park, an area around Garub, 20 km (about 12 miles) west of the desert town of Aus. In the last 20 years, however, the herds have suffered tremendously when drought struck the area.

Normally, the scant grasses and forage were enough to keep the small tribe of horses going, but even these could not grow in the drought years of 1991/2 and 1998/9, and many horses starved to death. When photos were released to the public of a skeletal horse on its death march in the desert, people rallied to the cause.

Equine and humanitarian organizations brought in food and water to the horses, ensuring that some of them would survive. Welfare groups arrived and installed troughs and feeding stations in parts of the desert. Other groups tried to round up the horses in order to care for them. These methods met with only limited success.

Park conservationists, looking at the global picture, came up with a plan to remove the horses from the park for the sake of their own continued survival, as well as that of the indigenous animals and flora. This met with such a loud outcry from the public and even from within the ministry, that the plan was dropped. The horses began to be promoted as a tourist attraction within the park and have actually boosted the park's economy. The horses were allowed to remain.

BELOW *Organizations have brought in troughs of water that help all wildlife get through severe droughts.*

Stepping in

The horses' problems are far from over. The debate still rages about whether the horses' presence in the desert is actually harming the native plants and other wildlife. The tourism ministry and several tour and travel organizations met to take up the debate, and a South African biologist conducted several studies, which proved inconclusive and failed to substantiate the claim that the horses displace the native flora and fauna.

In fact, there is little or no evidence of competition between the horses and the game animals, which occasionally graze within a few metres of each other without any apparent interaction. Gemsbok usually move away from the waterhole when the horses approach, and vice versa, but sometimes both species drink at the same time.

Therefore, the meeting looked at ways of managing the herds, rather than just coming to their aid during hard times.

They decided that the horses should not be regarded as game animals, such as the gemsbok and springbok. While the horses live in the wild – and therefore must deal with whatever nature throws its way, people also have to take some responsibility. For example, fencing has blocked off watering holes

BELOW *Some rain in spring gives the horse more plentiful grazing areas.*

ABOVE *The unique home that these horses have in the Namibian desert adds to their value as a tourist attraction.*

and good grazing for all wildlife and has also affected the number of gemsbok. In addition, during a drought, the numbers of horses could be so reduced that they end up becoming dangerously inbred.

The meeting agreed on a number of goals:

1 to ensure a stable population of wild horses

2 to keep the costs of their care as low as possible

3 to try to utilize the horses more efficiently as a tourist attraction

4 to gather more information on the animals

5 to improve the public's knowledge of the horses.

A prerequisite for controlling the horse population is the regular monitoring of rainfall, the availability of forage and the numbers and condition of the animals. The reference value for a stable population was set at 130, with short-term fluctuations between 80 and 180 regarded as acceptable.

The team of experts also recommended setting up watering places in neighbouring grazing areas in times of drought in order to shorten the horses' journey to find water, even though the horses are adapted to arid conditions and can go without water for longer than domestic horses, and without stress. However, the greater the distance they have to travel between their grazing area and water, the more energy they expend. The team also decided to make food available if the horses' condition began to seriously deteriorate. Young horses could be rounded up and removed from the herd to help keep numbers down.

The Namib wild horse today

Some progress has already been made in reaching the third goal, namely, to utilize the horses more efficiently as a tourist attraction. Today, visitors to the area can not only watch the horses from the shelter at the drinking trough near Garub, but, since mid-2006, they can also obtain all the background information on the horses at the Aus Information Centre, just 20 km (about 12 miles) away. This centre serves as a valuable source of income for the community of Aus and, at some stage in the more distant future, it could end up being combined with a wild horse research centre. The results of the research undertaken there could thus be passed on to visitors from Namibia and abroad.

Although their origins remain a mystery, the Namib wild horses are unique because of their isolation, their unique gene pool and the fact that they are able to survive in a climate that would kill most ordinary horses. Their ability to survive by changing their behaviour, and the way they conserve and expend energy, is a tremendous display of the enduring adaptability of the horse.

AUSTRALASIA

BRUMBY

AN UNEASY LIFE FOR AUSTRALIA'S WILD HORSES

In a scene as if from a film, a band of wild Brumbies gallops purposefully across the Northern Territory, led by the boss mare. They leap fallen trees, deftly avoid the rocks and, as one, fling themselves down a sheer mountainside. Without missing a step, they stride down the steep incline, a surging mass of horseflesh, to the valley floor. Within moments, they are gone.

First arrivals

The first horses to land on Australian shores, in 1788, were of English descent and came from South Africa. It was a long, arduous journey from the Cape of Good Hope, and some of the horses fell ill on the ships – weakened from the constant motion, the bad air in the cargo hold and the mouldering feed. Many horses, called 'Capers', died en route, and only the hardiest survived to put a hoof on Australian soil. These horses, with their tough constitution and spirit, did well in their new home.

Twenty years later, horse-racing became popular 'down under' and, in 1810, it became a recognized sport. As a result, top-quality English Thoroughbreds found their way to Australia. Horses were also imported from Chile, as were Timor ponies from Indonesia, and ponies and draught horses, such as the Clydesdale and Suffolk Punch, from the UK. Even Arabians found their way to Australia.

These horses helped to settle the Australian colony. The settlers used them to start farms and ranches, turning arid parts of the country into fertile land.

LEFT *Brumbies have many challenges ahead as they fight to co-exist successfully with humankind.*

ABOVE *When too many Brumbies are present, herds are gathered in 'musters' to be sold off; some, however, are destroyed.*

Explorers and traders used horses to cover the long distances. The finer-bred horses were used for racing and as carriage horses and saddle horses.

Because of the large open spaces of Australia, and the lack of fencing on the larger farms and ranches, many horses simply wandered off. Over the years, they were joined by other horses of various breeds and backgrounds. As agriculture became more mechanized, and in some desert and grassland areas where the horse was replaced by the camel, some horses were abandoned by their owners to run with the 'wild mobs', as these herds were called. These horses became known as wild Brumbies.

The mystery of its name

There are several theories as to how the feral horse of Australia became known as a Brumby. Some people believe that it owes its name to a soldier named James Brumby, who travelled to Australia on the ship *Britannia* in 1791. In addition to being a soldier, Brumby was also a farrier and took care of many horses in the New South Wales Corps. In 1804, when he left his home in Mulgrave Place, in New South Wales, to move to Tasmania, he left his horses behind. It is said that these horses were referred to as 'Brumby's horses'.

Others, however, turn to the native people for the origin of the name. In the Aboriginal language of the Pitjara the word for 'wild' is *baroomby*. Poet Banjo Paterson noted in the introduction to his poem 'Brumby's Run' that the word meant 'free-roaming horse'.

Yet another explanation points to Baramba, a creek and a cattle station in the Queensland district of Burnett. The station was established in the 1840s and later abandoned, leaving many of the horses to find their way in the wild. Finally, there are some people who claim that the name comes from the Gaelic word *bromach*, or *bromaigh*, meaning 'colt'.

Brumbies are found all over Australia, with the largest number living in the Northern Territory and the second largest in Queensland. However, when most people think of Brumbies, it is usually of the ones that live in the Australian Alps in the south-eastern part of the country.

A cunning mixture

While there is not really any one type of Brumby, because of the many different breeds and types of horses that have been introduced into the wild over the years, all Brumbies share a good deal of cunning, surefootedness, hardiness and intelligence.

They are found in all coat colours and patterns, including spotted Appaloosa patterns. While they vary in size, most are in the 14.2–15.2 hands (147.5–157.5 cm/58–62 in) range.

The problem with Brumbies

Although the Brumby has been romanticized in films and poetry, at the same time it has been reviled by some of the people with whom it shares the land. There are more feral horses living in Australia – roaming freely through the bush and the mountains – than anywhere else. This has been both a blessing and a curse for the Brumby.

As numbers grew – particularly in national parkland – many Brumbies were gathered in 'musters', to be caught and tamed for use on cattle and sheep stations. However, not everyone believed that the Brumby would be good to use. Brumbies have been one of the most hated feral horses in the world. Detractors argue that the horses are 'good for nothing', eat pasture intended for cattle, foul up good watering holes, destroy fencing, and make cattle-mustering tougher. They also often breed with domestic mares, which can spread disease to the domestic population.

BELOW *Horse lovers find the Brumby beautiful; its detractors find nothing to like about the so-called 'pests'.*

Culling

This led to culling of the herds. Proponents of culling say that it is necessary in order to reduce the horses' numbers so that they do not impact on the cattle ranches. In addition, they argue that it is for the greater good of the horses themselves because, when feed and water are scarce, they may suffer a slow death from starvation. And most say that the horses need to be removed because they damage the fragile ecosystems and native plants that other truly wild animals need to survive.

However, opponents of culling say that the practice is often carried out in an inhumane way, and that organizations should instead be trying to find other areas where the horses can live without interfering with human needs. They strongly believe that helicopter-mustering – the herding of horses from the air – is traumatic for the horse.

A tragic incident

Between 22 and 24 October 2000, in the Guy Fawkes River National Park, more than 600 Brumbies were brutally shot and killed – or left to die – in a major cull. This incident horrified animal-lovers across the globe and was the catalyst needed for animal-welfare advocates.

The National Parks and Wildlife Service (NPWS) carried out the aerial slaughter, in which horses were ineptly shot from helicopters. People were outraged to discover that many horses, allegedly culled humanely, suffered from their wounds for several days before dying. Many felt it was ironic

BELOW *Brumbies are found in many shapes, sizes and colours, including cremello, or cream, with blue eyes.*

ABOVE *An advocacy group, Save The Brumbies, draws some of its ideas from the management of mustangs in America, by the Bureau of Land Management.*

because, during the 2000 Olympic Games in Sydney, only months before, Australia had gone 'horse-crazy' when the country's team reigned supreme in one of the equestrian disciplines.

Even the Royal Society for the Prevention of Cruelty to Animals (RSPCA) took action against the NPWS, charging them with cruelty; their inspectors discovered a grey mare, barely alive 13 days after the culling, suffering with three bullets inside her. The case was settled in court: the NPWS pleaded guilty.

The Brumby today

A group called Save The Brumbies (STB) formed to lobby for changes in feral horse population management. Many Australians, as well as horse-lovers the world over, want to see the Brumbies protected. STB represents numerous horse interest groups, including the Australian Horse Alliance on the NPWS Steering Committee, that wish to find humane ways of Brumby control. They want to abolish shooting as a form of population control, and instead want sanctuaries set up so that the horses can run free.

Under current Department of Environment and Conservation legislation all wild horses are to be removed from national parks and government land. There has been no provision for their ongoing protection. The STB receives no funding or assistance from the government.

The Horse Management Plan for Guy Fawkes River National Park has been completed; however, shooting to cull the herds is still an option for control, despite protests.

After capture, Brumbies are often sold into the European horsemeat market – to France, Belgium and Italy – and also to Japan. Tragically, horses rounded up in musters are consigned to abattoirs or shot in the parks if horse interest groups do not have the land or finance to take them.

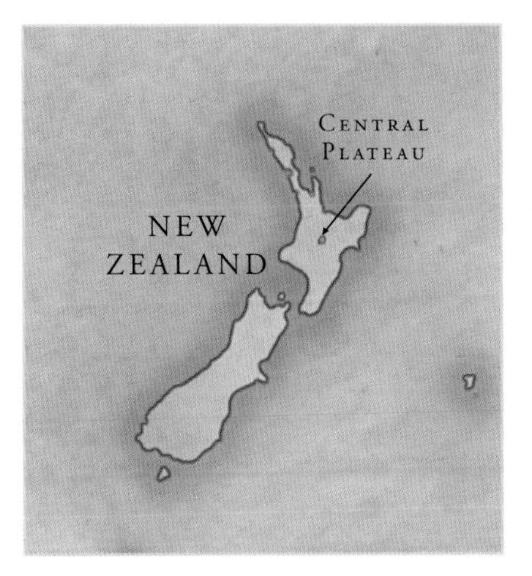

KAIMANAWA *wild horse*

NEW ZEALAND'S WILD HORSE

The Maori word *kaimanawa* translates as 'eat the wind'. This saying means that the brave will find a way to survive alone when resources are few and the future is uncertain and, in this way, they will endure. It is a fitting name for New Zealand's wild horse.

Eat the wind

While the Kaimanawa wild horse shows a lot of variation, in general, it is strong, smart and robust, either pony- or horse-sized (12.2–15 hands, or 127–152.5 cm/50–60 in), and comes in all coat patterns and colours. It has a medium-sized head, wide-set eyes and a short neck. The shoulder is straight and the body has a deep girth, with a medium-length back and a well-sprung rib cage. The croup is either rounded or sloping. The tail is medium-set and the hooves are hard and well formed. The horse has keen eyesight and hearing, is surefooted and can survive on meagre forage. It is also known for having excellent stamina.

The generations of New Zealand's wild horse

There were no horses at all in New Zealand until the 19th century, when, in December 1814, the Protestant clergyman Samuel Marsden imported horses to the islands. These quickly became a foundation stock.

About 40 years later, George Gwavas Carlyon, a major in the British army, introduced Exmoor ponies to the islands. Cross-breeding with the original stock resulted in the Carlyon pony, a sturdy, nimble little equine. Over

LEFT *Inquisitive but wary, the Kaimanawa makes a good riding horse when it has been tamed.*

generations, Welsh pony stallions were added to the mix, and a new breed was born: the Comet, a burlier powerhouse of a small horse.

The Comet became a favourite of riders working on sheep stations, because of its size, strength and willing temperament. Because it was also an attractive pony, the Comet was even exported to South Africa and Australia as a saddle pony and a carriage pony.

Sir Donald McLean, the original breeder of the Comets, released a single stallion into a band of mares on to the Kaingaroa Plains in the 1870s. They began a life of freedom and found their way into the Kaimanawa Mountains. In 1876, it was recorded that wild horses had indeed found their way off the plains and into the hills.

Additions to the mix

As in most populations of feral horses, plenty of different horses added to the mix, from Thoroughbreds to Arabians, as various breeds either escaped or were turned loose and abandoned to live in the wild. Some came from nearby sheep stations while others were turned loose by mounted rifle cavalry during the 1940s – for fear that they might be carriers of strangles, a disease that threatened the entire mounted forces.

With so many different horses being introduced, the Comet ceased to exist as a wild horse. Instead, the horses of the feral population grew a little taller and lankier, losing their diminutive stature and stocky build. However, 'throwbacks' – horses that exhibit traits of their forebears – can still be found

BELOW *Many different types of horse can be seen in one herd of Kaimanawas.*

ABOVE *Like the Brumbies, the Kaimanawas were rounded up to sell off when their numbers swelled.*

in the herd, even today. The main (and only remaining) herds found their final homes in the North Island's Central Plateau, where they became known as the Kaimanawa wild horses.

The Kaimanawa and the Maori

The existence of wild horses in New Zealand meant a great step forward for the native Maori people, transforming their society by giving them new freedom, power and opportunity from the back of a horse. The Maori captured the wild horses and used them for transport, in battle, and to work the land.

One Maori *hapu* (a family community within a tribe) regards the wild horse as a *kaitiaki* (a spiritual guardian) over its lands and its people. Each *hapu* has four *kaitiaki*, who protect the four corners of its boundaries, and the wild horse protects the northern boundary.

Hard times for the Kaimanawa

In the 1970s civilization began to encroach on the horses' habitat, and musters were held to round up the horses, mostly to sell them off to be slaughtered for pet food. The robust population took a downward turn.

Above *The Kaimanawa are often the target of environmentalists who see them as a danger to the native flora and fauna.*

Increasing concern for the horses resulted in a committee being formed in 1978, under the umbrella of the Forest Service, to look after the horses' interests. In 1981 a reserve was established, and the horses were given protected status under the Wildlife Act.

The Kaimanawa horses were then listed by the Food and Agricultural Organization of the United Nations, in Rome, as a herd of special genetic value, although plenty of people opposed this registration. They wanted the listing reviewed, claiming that the breed was not genetically unique.

Fortunately, as a result of the listing and the reserve, the population of horses rebounded with gusto and, by the mid-1990s, the numbers had risen from 200 to more than 1,000. Of course, this meant that individuals once again started to speak up against the horses – this time because they believed the horses were having a negative impact on the fragile ecosystem that they shared with other wildlife and on the delicate – and often endangered – indigenous plants. Opponents of the horses also noted that horses wandering on to roads were often involved in traffic accidents, endangering both themselves and humans.

The Kaimanawa Wild Horse Preservation Society was therefore formed in April 1994 to promote the preservation and protection of the Kaimanawa wild horse, both wild in the Kaimanawa Ranges and in domesticity. However, soon afterwards, the Department of Conservation (DOC) started looking critically at the horses, insisting that they were a threat to native plants and the animals that depended on them. It created a plan for managing the wild horses, which was adopted by parliament in May 1996. This included lifting their 'protected' status and a proposal to cull the horses by shooting from helicopters.

Results of public outcry

The public outcry was so strong that the government reversed its decision and, instead, allowed the horses to be mustered and auctioned to the public. Eventually a compromise was reached, with input from the DOC, Forest & Bird, the Society for the Prevention of Cruelty to Animals (SPCA), the Army and equine welfare organizations. They agreed that the horses would be removed from the northern two-thirds of their range, where the most delicate ecosystems and native flora were located, and a limit of 500 horses could live in the southern part of the range.

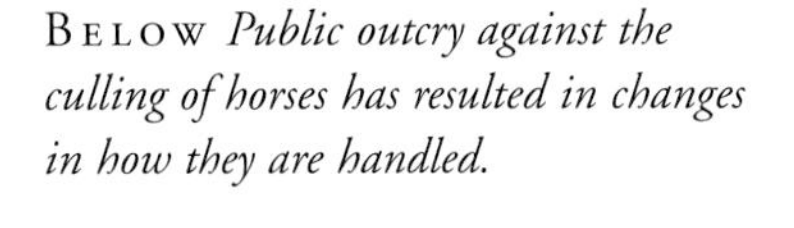

BELOW *Public outcry against the culling of horses has resulted in changes in how they are handled.*

The first round-up did not go as well as planned, however, because it was difficult to place a thousand feral horses with new owners. As a result, hundreds were slaughtered for horsemeat, to be shipped to Europe. However, their situation continues to improve, as fewer horses need to be rounded up each year. Whereas there were more than a thousand horses in the first round-up, there were less than 200 in subsequent years.

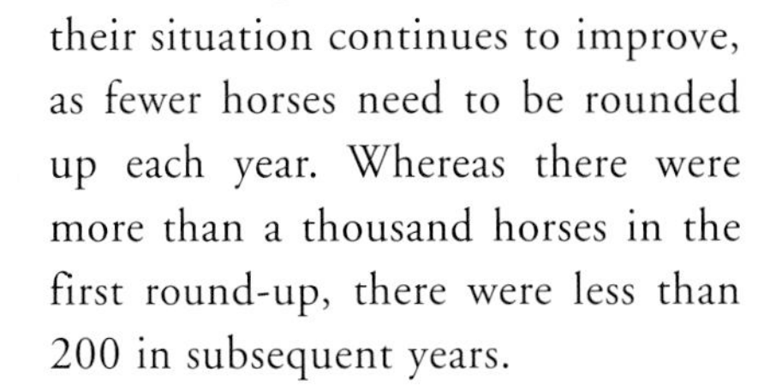

The habitat of the horses is also currently showing some signs of improvement, which is good news for all. The fencing-off of selected areas has demonstrated clearly that plant life will slowly rejuvenate. Furthermore, the proponents of the wild horse as a domestic partner are also helping the breed's image; thus they are being recognized more as good mounts, rather than just pests. It is this, coupled with the vigilance of their supporters that will help to ensure a more certain future for the Kaimanawa.

INDEX

Figures in italics indicate captions.

Acknowledgements

Executive Editor Trevor Davies
Editor Amy Corbett
Executive Art Editor Leigh Jones
Design Miranda Harvey
Senior Production Controller Linda Parry
Photography Bob Langrish

Photography Bob Langrish
with the exception of the following:
6 courtesy of HRH The Princess Royal; 16 Cécile Domens & Richard Fasseur; 17 FLPA/ImageBroker; 20 FLPA/David Hosking; 21 FLPA/Konrad Wothe/Minden Pictures; 22, 24, 26, 27 above & below Sable Island Green Horse Society/Zoe Lucas; 150, 152, 153 www.panbike.com/Pantelis Ioannidis; 158, 162, 164, 166 Cécile Domens & Richard Fasseur; 184, 186 Kit Houghton; 187 Getty Images/Ross Land; 188, 189 robtucker.co.nz